"Morris Goldstein makes a powerful argument for the rapid adoption of an International Banking Standard—and he tells us precisely what needs to be done, by whom, and when. This is reasoned public advocacy at its best."
Stanley Fischer, First Deputy Managing Director, International Monetary Fund

"Banking crises have often imposed enormous costs on the countries in which they have occurred. As a result, the importance of making national banking systems more resilient is now widely endorsed. How can this be achieved? This thoughtful and occasionally provocative analysis by one of the most astute observers of the field could not be more timely."
Andrew Crockett, General Manager, Bank for International Settlements

"The interface of stabilization-induced recession and high interest rates with financial deregulation has produced banking crises around the world. The conspicuous problem is not bad luck but rather a lack of supervision and suitable standards. High time, therefore, to give ample discussion to this proposal by Morris Goldstein that highlights a gaping hole in international financial cooperation and how to fill it. An important book and a brilliant accomplishment. A must for ministers of finance, the financial industry, and investors alike."
Rudi Dornbusch, Ford Professor of Economics, MIT

"An excellent study—timely and thoroughly researched; makes a valuable contribution to the ongoing debate."
Robert Litan, Director of Economic Studies, Brookings Institution

MORRIS GOLDSTEIN

The Case for an International Banking Standard

Institute for International Economics
Washington, DC
April 1997

Morris Goldstein, *Dennis Weatherstone Senior Fellow,* held several senior staff positions at the International Monetary Fund (1970-94), including Deputy Director of its Research Department (1987-94). He has written extensively on international economic policy and on international capital markets. He is coeditor of *Private Capital Flows to Emerging Markets after the Mexican Crisis* (1996), author of *The Exchange Rate System and the IMF: A Modest Agenda* (1995), and coauthor of "Banking Crises in Emerging Economies" (BIS, 1996), "The Integration of World Capital Markets" (Federal Reserve Bank of Kansas City, 1994), *Exchange Rate Management and International Capital Flows* (IMF, 1993), "The Macroeconomic Implications of Currency Zones" (Federal Reserve Bank of Kansas City, 1992), and *International Policy Coordination and Exchange Rate Fluctuations* (NBER, 1990).

INSTITUTE FOR INTERNATIONAL ECONOMICS
11 Dupont Circle, NW
Washington, DC 20036-1207
(202) 328-9000   FAX: (202) 328-5432
http://www.iie.com

C. Fred Bergsten, *Director*

Christine F. Lowry, *Director of Publications*

Typesetting and Printing by Automated Graphic Systems

Printed in the United States of America
99 98 97   5 4 3 2 1

Library of Congress Cataloging-in-Publication Data

Goldstein, Morris, 1944-
The case for an international banking standard / Morris Goldstein.
p. cm.—(Policy analyses in international economics : 47)Includes bibliographical references.
1. Banks and banking, International. 2. Banks and banking, International--Developing countries. I. Title. II. Series.
HG3881.G61435 1997   97-5475
332.1′5--dc21   CIP

ISBN 0-88132-244-X

The views expressed in this publication are those of the author. This publication is part of the overall program of the Institute, as endorsed by its Board of Directors, but does not necessarily reflect the views of individual members of the Board or the Advisory Committee.

Contents

Appendices

Preface

The Institute has done extensive work over the years on financial crises. We published several studies by William Cline on the Third World debt crisis of the 1980s, ranging from his initial analysis in 1983 (*International Debt and the Stability of the World Economy*) through his reappraisal in 1995 of the entire episode (*International Debt Reexamined*). John Williamson's *Voluntary Approaches to Debt Relief* (1988) made a major contribution to the midcourse correction of the systemic response to that problem. We recently released *Private Capital Flows to Emerging Markets after the Mexican Crisis*, edited by Guillermo Calvo, Morris Goldstein, and Eduard Hochreiter, which analyzes the lessons and policy implications of the latest round of global financial instability.

This new study by Morris Goldstein, the Dennis Weatherstone Senior Fellow at the Institute, marks our first foray into the area of international banking supervision and regulation. In it, Dr. Goldstein presents the case for an international banking standard (IBS). The motivation is easy to explain. During the past 15 years there has been an epidemic of banking crises in the developing world. Nearly three-fourths of all countries have experienced at least one serious bout of banking problems during this period. In at least 57 instances the banking system's capital has been wholly or almost exhausted. In more than a dozen cases the costs of reducing these crises have amounted to 10 percent or more of the country's GDP. And the total public-sector tab of resolving banking crises in all developing countries has been estimated to total at least $250 billion.

These banking crises are not only extremely costly to the developing countries themselves. These countries now account for 36 percent of global inflows of foreign direct investment, 30 percent of global portfolio flows, 11 to 13 percent of global banking assets, and 11 percent of global stock market capitalization. Hence, their crises pose a risk to industrial countries and the entire world economy as well. These spillovers and the significant banking problems suffered by industrial countries themselves over this period (including, inter alia, the massive ongoing bad loan problem in Japan and the earlier saving and loan debacle in the United States) provide ample reason for industrial countries to also support an IBS.

Dr. Goldstein shows that existing international banking agreements, designed primarily from the perspective of the industrial countries, do not address the major factors behind banking crises in developing countries. These factors include: excessive government involvement in and public ownership of the banking industry; weak disclosure, accounting, and legal frameworks; too much lending to bank owners, managers, and their affiliated companies (so-called connected lending); inadequate bank capital relative to the volatile macroeconomic environment; and official safety nets that do not give bank owners and creditors enough to lose when they bring a bank to insolvency and do not provide enough institutional protection against strong political pressures for regulatory forbearance.

The author argues that an IBS, open to developing and industrial countries alike, is the most promising way to motivate serious banking reform. Although subscription to an IBS would be voluntary, market participants' knowledge of who is or is not participating would establish a market premium for joining. In addition, the official sector could supplement this incentive by allowing IBS participation to influence the terms and conditions for loans from the IMF and the World Bank.

The author emphasizes that earlier agreements on international standards or guidelines in financial markets—including the IMF's Special Data Dissemination Standard, the Group of Thirty's guidelines on both trading and settlement of securities and risk management of derivatives, and the Basle Committee's Capital Adequacy Accord—have produced encouraging results. Countries have found that such international standards offer them incentives to make improvements that are absent or weaker if they act unilaterally—either because of competitive pressures or lack of credibility.

Dr. Goldstein then answers several key operational questions that would arise under an IBS, including: What individual supervisory/regulatory guidelines should an IBS include? How would compliance with the guidelines be monitored and encouraged? He maintains that the highest priority should be accorded to eight guidelines, covering public disclosure of banks' financial condition, the accounting and legal framework, internal controls at banks, government involvement in the banking system, connected lending, bank capital, the design of the official safety net, and cooperation among host- and home-country banking supervisors. He proposes an action agenda for reaching agreement on an IBS by the time of the annual meetings of the International Monetary Fund and World Bank in Hong Kong in September 1997.

Dr. Goldstein's ideas for an IBS have been circulating in official circles for almost a year, and his views have already played a major role in the policy debate. Action proposals are now being developed by the Basle Committee on Banking Supervision, the IMF, and a G-10/developing country working group of finance and central bank deputies. The issue is likely to be discussed intensively in G-7 and IMF meetings over the next six months. Dr. Goldstein's own proposals offer a benchmark against which to judge official-sector proposals—to see whether the official sector is meeting the formidable challenges faced by banking authorities in emerging-market countries and lowering the risks those challenges pose to the global economy.

The Institute for International Economics is a private nonprofit institution for the study and discussion of international economic policy. Its purpose is to analyze important issues in that area and to develop and communicate practical new approaches for dealing with them. The Institute is completely nonpartisan.

The Institute is funded largely by philanthropic foundations. Major institutional grants are now being received from The German Marshall Fund of the United States, which created the Institute with a substantial commitment of funds in 1981, and from The Ford Foundation, The Andrew W. Mellon Foundation, and The C. V. Starr Foundation. A number of other foundations and private corporations also contribute to the highly diversified financial resources of the Institute. The Rockefeller Brothers Fund provided substantial support for this study. About 16 percent of the Institute's resources in our latest fiscal year were provided by contributors outside the United States, including about 7 percent from Japan.

The Board of Directors bears overall responsibility for the Institute and gives general guidance and approval to its research program—including identification of topics that are likely to become important to international economic policymakers over the medium run (generally, one to three years), and which thus should be addressed by the Institute. The Director, working closely with the staff and outside Advisory Committee, is responsible for the development of particular projects and makes the final decision to publish an individual study.

The Institute hopes that its studies and other activities will contribute to building a stronger foundation for international economic policy around the world. We invite readers of these publications to let us know how they think we can best accomplish this objective.

C. FRED BERGSTEN
Director
April 1997

Acknowledgments

I am indebted to a group of colleagues for their support and advice in preparing this study. Both the Bank for International Settlements (BIS) and the International Monetary Fund (IMF) provided excellent opportunities for me to learn more about developing-country banking problems during my time there as a visiting scholar. At the BIS, special thanks go to Andrew Crockett, Philip Turner, and Bill White; similarly, I am particularly grateful to Stanley Fischer, David Folkerts-Landau, Mohsin Khan, and Michael Mussa at the IMF. In addition, the following individuals made helpful suggestions on all or part of an earlier draft of this paper: George Benston, Gerry Caprio, Peter Dittus, Rudi Dornbusch, Richard Herring, Patrick Honohan, Ed Kane, George Kaufman, Peter Kenen, Ruth Krivoy, Carl Lindgren, Robert Litan, Kevin O'Connor, Tommaso Padoa-Schioppa, Carmen Reinhart, Alice Rivlin, Liliana Rojas-Suarez, William Seidman, Jeff Shafer, Andrew Sheng, Ted Truman, John Williamson, and Rick Zechter. In addition to offering his valuable comments on the entire manuscript, C. Fred Bergsten could not have been more encouraging of my efforts over the past year to develop the rationale for, and the design of, an international banking standard. Also here at the Institute, I am grateful to Neal Luna for superb research assistance, and to Brigitte Coulton, Helen Kim, David Krzywda, and Christine Lowry for getting the published version ready under such a tight deadline. I of course remain solely responsible for any errors and omissions that remain.

1

Introduction

This study presents the case for an international banking standard (IBS). An IBS would go beyond existing international banking agreements to better address the factors underlying the rash of banking crises that has afflicted developing countries over the past 15 years. An IBS would also help to improve banking supervision in industrial countries.

Chapter 2 outlines the case for an IBS. It emphasizes that during the past 15 years banking crises in developing countries have been widespread and severe. Such banking crises have been costly for the countries involved and increasingly pose risks to others. Existing international agreements do not confront the main origins of banking crises in developing countries, and a voluntary IBS offers a more attractive route to banking reform than the alternatives.

Chapter 3 takes up four key operational questions associated with the design and implementation of an IBS:

- Should there be a unitary standard that applies to all countries, or should an IBS have two levels?

- What guidelines should be included in an IBS?

- Who would set the standard?

- How would compliance with the standard be monitored and encouraged?

In answering these operational questions, several potential criticisms of an IBS are also evaluated.

Chapter 4 offers brief concluding remarks, including an action agenda for reaching an IBS agreement by the September 1997 Annual Meetings of the International Monetary Fund and World Bank in Hong Kong, if not sooner. Finally, four appendices provide supplementary material: on the location and timing of developing-country banking problems; on several examples of earlier international financial standards; on differences among industrial countries as regards permissible banking activities, bank ownership, and banking supervisory practices; and on possible formats for public disclosure of banks' financial condition.

2

The Problem and Why
an IBS Is Needed

The Frequency and Severity of Banking Crises

The recent history of banking crises points to a striking finding: *during the past 15 years, banking crises in developing countries have been unusually frequent and severe*—relative to both their own record during the preceding three decades and to experience in industrial countries (Caprio and Klingebiel 1996a, 1996b; Honohan 1996; Kaminsky and Reinhart 1995; Lindgren, Garcia, and Saal 1996; Sheng 1996; Sundararajan and Baliño 1991).

According to Lindgren, Garcia, and Saal (1996), 73 percent of the International Monetary Fund's (IMF) member countries experienced at least one bout of significant banking-sector problems from 1980 to 1996.[1] In Africa, Asia, and the transition economies of Central and Eastern Europe, this figure rises to more than 90 percent. Appendix A details the countries and time periods involved.

As to the severity of banking crises, bank losses or public-sector resolution costs amounted to 10 percent or more of GDP in at least a dozen developing-country episodes during the past 15 years. Table 2.1, adapted from Caprio and Klingebiel (1996a), lists these severe banking crises.

---

1. Lindgren, Garcia, and Saal (1996) define banking crises as cases where there were bank runs or other substantial portfolio shifts, collapses of financial firms, or massive government intervention. They use the adjective "significant" to describe extensive banking-sector unsoundness short of a crisis. Using this methodology, they classify 41 episodes (in 36 countries) as crises, and another 108 episodes as significant banking-sector problems. As a whole, the identification of banking crises is quite consistent across different studies.

Table 2.1 Severe banking crises, 1980–96

Country (time period of crisis)	Estimate of total losses/costs (percentage of GDP)
Latin America	
Argentina (1980–82)	55
Chile (1981–83)	41[a]
Venezuela (1994–95)	18
Mexico (1995)	12–15[b]
Africa	
Benin (1988–90)	17
Cote d'Ivoire (1988–91)	25
Mauritania (1984–93)	15
Senegal (1988–91)	17
Tanzania (1987–95)	10[c]
Middle East	
Israel (1977–83)	30[d]
Transition countries	
Bulgaria (1990s)	14
Hungary (1995)	10
Industrial countries	
Spain (1977–85)	17
Japan (1990s)	10[e]

a. 1982–85.
b. accumulated loses to date.
c. in 1987.
d. in 1983.
e. estimate of potential losses.

Source: Caprio and Klingebiel (1996a).

Employing the less demanding definition of a crisis as an exhaustion of all or most of the banking system's capital, Caprio and Klingebiel (1996a) find that there have been 67 such crises since 1980, involving 52 developing countries; moreover, this clearly represents a lower bound on the true number of developing-country banking crises, since information for many of the transition economies was not available.

One recent study by Honohan (1996) estimated that resolution costs of banking crises in developing and transition economies since 1980 have approached $250 billion.[2] While industrial countries have had some nota-

---

2. Honohan (1996) arrives at this figure using a two-step procedure. In the first step, he regresses resolution costs of banking crises on the share of nonperforming loans, using a sample of developing countries for which data on both variables are available. In the second step, he uses that estimated regression to predict resolution costs for those developing countries where only data on nonperforming loans are available.

ble banking crises of their own over this period (Spain, 1977-85; Finland, Norway, and Sweden, in the late 1980s/early 1990s; and the current Japanese bad loan problem), they have typically been less severe (relative to GDP) than in developing countries.[3] For example, the US saving and loan debacle of 1984-91 (with an estimated resolution cost of two to three percent of GDP) does not even make Caprio and Klingebiel's (1996a) global list of systemic banking crises; instead, it becomes grouped with other borderline and smaller banking crises.[4]

The recent wave of banking crises in developing countries apparently does not reflect a return to the incidence of crises in earlier periods; historical studies can find no historical precedent for the last quarter century's dismal track record of banking problems (Honohan 1996).[5] Within the last 25 years, the frequency of banking crises among emerging economies and smaller industrial countries has been much higher during the 1980s and 1990s than during the 1970s.[6]

The Costs of Banking Crises: Impact on Local Economies and Potential Spillover Effects to Industrial Countries

A second important finding is that *banking crises are costly for the local economies involved* (Bank for International Settlements [BIS] 1996; Caprio and Klingebiel 1996b; Goldstein and Turner 1996; Lindgren, Garcia, and Saal 1996). In addition, *the increasing weight and integration of emerging economies in international financial markets have made potential spillover effects to industrial and to other developing countries a more relevant concern* (BIS 1996; Goldstein and Turner 1996; G-10 1996).

---

3. As illustrated in table 2.1, the Spanish banking crisis of 1977-85 is an exception to this general proposition; the Japanese banking crisis of the 1990s may also, in the end, have resolution costs (relative to GDP) that are high by industrial-country standards. Caprio and Klingebiel (1996a) place the resolution costs of the Finnish (1991-93), Swedish (1991), and Norwegian (1987-89) banking problems at 8, 6, and 4 percent of GDP, respectively.

4. Similarly, Lindgren, Garcia, and Saal (1996) classify the US saving and loan problem as a significant banking problem but not as a crisis.

5. Although the 1950-75 period was an unusually tranquil one in terms of banking failures, Honohan (1996) makes some rough comparisons with periods and episodes prior to 1950 to support his claim that recent bank crashes are unprecedented in terms of their size and frequency.

6. In their sample of 20 emerging economies and smaller industrial countries, Kaminsky and Reinhart (1995) find that the average annual frequency of banking crises has climbed from 0.3 in the 1970s to 1.4 in the 1980-95 period.

Table 2.2 Role of banks in financial intermediation in developing countries, 1994

Country	Bank share[a] in financial intermediation
India	80
Indonesia	91
Korea, South	38
Malaysia	64
Singapore	71
Taiwan	80
Thailand	75
Argentina	98
Brazil	97
Chile	62
Colombia	86
Mexico	87
Venezuela	92

a. Percentage of the assets of banks and nonbank financial institutions.

Source: Goldstein and Turner (1996).

Banks hold the lion's share of financial assets in developing countries (see table 2.2). Banks operate the payments system, provide liquidity to fledgling securities markets, and are major purchasers of government bonds. And over the past two decades, bank liabilities have grown much faster than economic activity in developing countries (Honohan 1996). It is not surprising then that banking crises in developing countries are associated with large and wide-ranging negative externalities.

As indicated above, banking crises have been linked to massive government bailouts, making it more difficult to control fiscal deficits in developing countries.[7] But the costs for the local economies involved go well beyond the fiscal implications. Specifically, research suggests that banking crises exacerbate downturns in economic activity, prevent savings from flowing to its most productive use, reduce the availability and increase the cost of credit to small- and medium-sized firms, and seriously constrain the flexibility of monetary policy (including, among other things, the willingness to increase interest rates to deal with large, abrupt shifts in international capital flows) (Bernanke 1983; BIS 1996; Caprio and Klingebiel 1996b; De Gregorio and Guidotti 1992; Goldstein and Turner 1996; Kaminsky and Reinhart 1995; Lindgren, Garcia, and Saal 1996; Mishkin 1994).

---

7. See Edwards (1995) on how large-scale public bailouts of banks have handicapped efforts at fiscal consolidation in Latin America. Note that even if the fiscal costs of bank bailouts are viewed as simply a transfer payment, the way this transfer is financed (e.g., inflation or other taxes) can be costly (Honohan 1996; Caprio and Klingebiel 1996b).

Between 1991 and mid-1994, the share of nonperforming loans in Mexico's banking system increased from about 4 to 8 percent. Calvo and Goldstein (1996) have argued that banking-system fragility best explains why from April to December 1994 the Mexican authorities engaged in a large-scale substitution of lower-yielding dollar-indexed government securities *(tesobonos)* for higher-yielding peso-denominated ones *(cetes)* while acting to offset the effects of declining private capital inflows and international reserves on the money supply. These actions were aimed at limiting the rise in interest rates and buying time for the banks to recover. Yet, by thwarting the adjustment process, Mexican authorities magnified the fall in international reserves and turned a currency crisis into a debt crisis. So long as the local banking system is close to the edge, authorities will be responding to volatile private capital flows with one hand tied behind their backs.

Because developing countries are now larger importers, debtors, and recipients of international capital flows than they used to be, there is also an increased risk that banking crises in emerging economies will have unfavorable externalities on industrial countries (as well as other developing countries). Indeed, as will be emphasized, such spillovers provide one of the incentives for industrial-country support of an IBS.

Developing countries now account for approximately 45 percent of global output (using purchasing-power-parity weights), 36 percent of global foreign direct investment inflows, 30 percent of global portfolio capital flows, 11 percent of global stock market capitalization, 12 percent of global issuance of international bonds, and 11 to 13 percent of global banking assets (Barth, Nolle, and Rice 1996; IFC 1996; IMF 1995, 1996a; Quereshi 1996; World Bank 1997). Two of the world's six largest foreign exchange trading centers (Hong Kong and Singapore) are not G-10 countries (BIS 1996). By each of these indicators, the weight of developing countries in the global economy is considerably larger than it was 5 or 10 years ago.[8]

Industrial countries are increasingly affected by the economic fortunes of developing countries. The latter now purchase roughly 25 percent of industrial-country exports. From 1990 to 1996, developing countries received nearly $1.1 trillion in net private capital flows from industrial countries (IMF 1996a). By the end of 1995, banks in the BIS reporting area had over $717 billion in outstanding claims against developing-country banks ($46 billion more than their liabilities to these banks); moreover, there were some large net claims on banks in individual developing countries/territories (e.g., $215 billion on banks in Hong Kong, $117 billion on banks in Singapore, $68 billion on banks in Thailand, and $45 billion

---

8. For example, in 1990 the developing-country share of global foreign direct investment flows was roughly 15 percent, while its share of global portfolio equity flows was less than 2 percent (World Bank 1997).

on banks in Korea)(IMF 1996a).[9] Nonresidents reportedly held about 80 percent of the *tesobonos* outside the banking system at the time of the Mexican crisis (BIS 1995). From 1990 to 1994, more than 30 percent of new international investments by US mutual funds were directed at emerging markets, and by the end of 1995, US-based open-end mutual funds had approximately $36 billion invested in emerging markets. The analogous figure for US pension funds is estimated at $50-70 billion (World Bank 1997). Empirical studies indicate that banking crises in developing countries (as in the recent Mexican case) often are linked to subsequent currency crises (Kaminsky and Reinhart 1995), and the prominent role banks play in developing-country equity and bond markets suggests that these asset markets might also be affected. For example, bank stocks (in 1995) comprised 14 percent of the International Financing Corporation's (IFC) emerging-market composite equity index, and there are a number of emerging economies (e.g., Jordan, the Philippines, Poland, Portugal, Sri Lanka, and Thailand) where the financial sector (including insurance and real estate) had the largest share (typically exceeding 45 percent) of the local equity market's capitalization (IFC 1996). The Mexican crisis also revealed that the contagion of financial disturbances across developing countries can be marked, at least in the short term.[10]

As noted above, bank losses often become liabilities of developing-country governments. In turn, over the past 15 years, all IMF loans have gone to developing countries.

As table 2.3 shows, private credit-rating agencies continue to assess the likelihood that banks in developing countries might need financial assistance at significantly higher levels, on average, than in industrial countries. Whereas over 90 percent of the developing-country banks listed in table 2.3 fall into one of Moody's bottom-five financial strength rating categories, less than 40 percent of industrial-country banks do.

To be sure, the potential cross-border spillover effects of developing-country banking crises should be kept in perspective. Spillovers are not yet nearly as large as those that would be associated with banking crises in the major industrial countries (Herring and Litan 1995).[11] Some claims on developing countries are collateralized (e.g., repurchase agreements), and now that private capital flows to developing countries are comprised markedly less by bank loans and more by equity and bond flows, the investor base in industrial countries is better diversified than it was at the outbreak of the 1980s debt crisis (when US money-center banks found

---

9. The figures refer to net outstanding credit at year end 1995.

10. For evidence of such contagion, see IMF (1995) and Calvo and Reinhart (1996).

11. Whereas exposure to emerging markets has been growing rapidly over the past five years, US pension funds and mutual funds have only about 2 percent of their total assets invested in emerging markets (World Bank 1997).

Table 2.3 Moody's bank financial strength ratings: industrial versus developing countries, May 1996

	A	B+	B	C+	C	D+	D	E+	E	Total
Industrial Countries										
Australia	0	0	3	4	4	1	0	0	0	12
Austria	0	0	1	2	2	2	0	0	0	7
Belgium	0	2	2	2	1	0	0	0	0	7
Canada	0	1	5	4	0	0	0	0	0	10
Denmark	0	0	1	1	1	0	0	0	0	3
Finland	0	0	0	0	0	3	0	0	1	4
France	1	2	5	4	5	5	4	0	1	27
Germany	3	2	4	8	6	3	0	0	0	26
Hong Kong	0	0	2	0	5	0	0	0	0	7
Italy	0	0	3	6	4	2	0	1	2	18
Japan	0	0	3	0	10	9	17	7	3	49
Luxembourg	0	0	3	0	0	0	0	0	0	3
Netherlands	3	1	0	1	0	0	0	0	0	5
Norway	0	0	0	0	3	1	0	0	0	4
Spain	1	3	5	1	2	0	0	0	0	12
Sweden	0	0	0	1	4	0	0	0	0	5
Switzerland	1	2	1	1	1	1	0	0	0	7
United Kingdom	1	5	9	5	5	1	1	0	0	27
United States	3	21	68	113	80	11	0	0	0	296
Total	**13**	**42**	**115**	**154**	**135**	**39**	**22**	**8**	**7**	**535**
Developing countries										
Argentina	0	0	0	0	2	3	4	1	0	10
Brazil	0	0	0	2	1	8	3	1	2	17
Chile	0	0	0	4	3	3	0	0	0	10
China	0	0	0	0	0	1	1	3	0	5
Colombia	0	0	0	1	3	0	2	0	0	6
Czech Republic	0	0	0	0	0	2	2	1	0	5

(continued on next page)

their impaired claims on developing countries to be larger than their capital) (Cline 1995; World Bank 1997). Still, the potential spillover effects of developing-country banking crises are already far from trivial.[12] In addition, most analysts expect industrial- and developing-country financial interdependence to increase over the medium term.

Among the factors expected to drive increasing private capital flows to developing countries over the next decade are: relatively high expected

---

12. A recent report on sovereign liquidity crises by the Deputies of the G-10 (1996, iv) arrived at a similar conclusion: ". . . The Working Party recognized that structural weaknesses in the banking systems of debtor [developing] countries could seriously aggravate liquidity crises and pose difficulties for financial systems in lender [industrial] countries." Likewise, W. White (1996, 22) concludes that ". . . many emerging economies already have domestic financial systems of such a size that systemic problems locally could have important systemic effects internationally."

Table 2.3 (continued)

	A	B+	B	C+	C	D+	D	E+	E	Total
Hong Kong	0	0	2	0	5	0	0	0	0	7
Hungary	0	0	0	0	0	2	2	1	0	5
India	0	0	0	0	0	2	2	1	1	6
Indonesia	0	0	0	0	0	3	4	2	2	11
Korea	0	0	0	0	1	4	3	2	0	10
Malaysia	0	0	0	1	0	0	0	0	0	1
Mexico	0	0	0	0	0	0	3	4	2	9
Oman	0	0	0	0	0	3	1	0	0	4
Panama	0	0	0	0	1	0	0	0	0	1
Philippines	0	0	0	1	1	5	2	0	0	9
Poland	0	0	0	0	0	3	3	1	0	7
Singapore	0	3	0	1	2	0	0	0	0	6
South Africa	0	0	0	0	3	2	0	0	0	5
Taiwan	0	0	0	0	5	0	0	0	0	5
Thailand	0	0	0	2	1	1	3	0	0	7
Venezuela	0	0	0	0	0	2	3	0	0	5
Total	**0**	**3**	**2**	**12**	**28**	**44**	**38**	**17**	**7**	**151**

Note: As described in IMF (1996b), Moody's Investors Service introduced a new rating system for financial institutions in 1995, called the Bank Financial Strength Rating (BFSR). Whereas an institutions's long-term debt rating indicates the agency's assessment of the likelihood of default, the BFSR represents an opinion of a bank's intrinsic strength, or alternatively, the likelihood that the institution will require financial assistance from third parties such as its owners or the government. The BFSR does not incorporate the probability that such support will be forthcoming, only the probability that it will be needed. Hence, a bank may have a relatively low BFSR, but a higher long-term credit rating, reflecting the opinion that third-party support would be forthcoming to prevent a default. In arriving at the BFSR, Moody's considers the bank's financial fundamentals, its franchise value, its main risk factors, the macroeconomic environment, and the quality of banking regulation and supervision. Differences in average BFSRs across countries, therefore, could indicate relative weaknesses in the overall soundness of the banking system, due either to poor bank performance or inadequacies in the regulatory infrastructure.

Sources: Moody's Investors Source; IMF (1996b).

rates of return (based in part on projected growth rates of real output in the developing countries that are about twice as high as for the industrial countries), large untapped opportunities for risk diversification by industrial-country investors (optimal portfolio considerations suggest that the share of developing-country securities in the portfolios of industrial-country institutional investors should be at least four or five times greater than the existing share), globalization of production, growing liquidity and maturity of developing-country securities markets, growing importance of institutional investors, and liberalization and policy reform in developing countries.[13] As but one additional indicator of recent trends,

---

13. See World Bank (1997)

in 1992 there were 449 international emerging-market equity funds with $29 billion in net assets; by 1995, there were 1254 such funds with almost $109 billion in net assets.

Because banking crises in developing countries, inter alia, depress growth and foreign trade, strain debt-servicing capacity, and eventually often wind up as liabilities of developing-country governments, industrial countries too have a stake in promoting stronger banking systems in the developing world.

The Origins of Banking Crises in Developing Countries

If banking crises in developing countries[14] are pervasive and costly, what lies behind these crises? Recent research shows that *banking crises in developing countries have multiple origins.*

Developing-country banks operate within a more volatile environment than do their industrial-country counterparts. Volatility in the terms of trade, cost of borrowing on international markets, private capital flows, real exchange rates, and growth and inflation rates have been much higher on average during the past two decades in developing countries than in industrial countries.[15] Banks in those countries, therefore, face relatively high credit and market risk. Moreover, as I shall document later on banks in developing countries—with several notable exceptions—have not chosen to compensate for this higher risk either by holding significantly more capital than banks in the largest industrial countries, or by being more conserva-

---

14. The arguments summarized in this subsection are developed more fully in Goldstein and Turner (1996).

15. Hausman and Gavin (1995) estimate that over the past 20 years the standard deviation of changes in the terms of trade in Latin American emerging markets is about twice as high on average as in industrial countries. Caprio and Klingebiel (1996a) show that three-quarters of developing countries experiencing a banking crisis suffered at least a 10 percent decline in their terms of trade just prior to a banking crisis. Studies by Calvo, Leiderman, and Reinhart (1993) and Dooley, Fernandez-Arias, and Kletzer (1994) suggest that movements in international interest rates explain between one-half and two-thirds of the surge in private capital inflows to developing countries in the 1990s. Owing mainly to highly variable inflation rates, Hausman and Gavin (1995) report that the volatility of real exchange rates in Latin America has been about twice that of industrial countries over the past two decades. BIS (1996) and Hausman and Gavin (1995) document the greater volatility of growth and inflation rates in developing countries (vis-à-vis industrial countries) over the past 15 years; countries with the most variable growth and inflation performance also tend to display relatively high variability in bank deposits and bank credit growth (BIS 1996). Kaminsky and Reinhart (1995) provide evidence that recessions have been one of most reliable leading indicators of banking crises in developing countries. On the whole, the operating environment for banks has been more volatile in Latin American emerging economies than for Asian ones.

Table 2.4 Foreign-owned banks

Country	Percentage share of total assets
Hong Kong	78.0[a]
India	7.3
Indonesia	3.7
Korea	5.1
Malaysia	15.9
Singapore	80.0
Taiwan	4.7
Thailand	7.1
Argentina	21.7
Brazil	9.4
Chile	21.4
Colombia	3.6
Mexico	1.2
Venezuela	1.2
Russian Ferderation	2.2
Israel	0.0
South Africa	3.3
Germany	3.9
Japan	1.8
United States	22.0

Note: Figures refer to latest available year.

a. Refers to all overseas-incorporated authorized institutions.

Sources: OECD, central banks, ministries of finance, and Goldstein and Turner (1996).

tive in provisioning for bad loans. While some emerging economies have diversified in the face of local volatility by permitting a higher market share for foreign-owned banks,[16] many others have discouraged such a role for foreign banks (Dermine 1996).[17] Table 2.4 shows the percentage share of banking assets accounted for by foreign-owned banks in a group of developing countries.

In short, with low macroeconomic stability, limited diversification, and a relatively small financial cushion against large changes in the value of bank assets or liabilities (i.e., bank capital and loan-loss provisions), banks in many developing countries have been skating on thin ice.

---

16. This diversification arises because the portfolios of foreign-owned banks are less concentrated in lending to firms of the host country and because these banks have access to external sources of liquidity and foreign exchange (from their parents abroad) (Gavin and Hausman 1996a, 1996b).

17. In 1992, for example, Dermine (1996) reports that the permissible foreign ownership share was less than 30 percent (of voting rights) in Mexico, less than 20 percent in Malaysia, less than 10 percent in Korea, and less than 5 percent in Singapore.

Vulnerability has also been linked (especially in Latin America) to a *tendency for developing-country banks (like their industrial-country counterparts) to lend too freely during the upswing of the business cycle, with such lending booms stoked by large-scale capital inflows and made more fragile by an excessive concentration of credit in real estate and equity markets* (Gavin and Hausman 1996a; Mishkin 1994).[18] In addition, normal banking liquidity and maturity mismatches have frequently been magnified by a rapid expansion in bank liabilities, a short-term orientation of the financial system, and an excessive resort to foreign-currency denominated borrowing—all within a context of highly variable international reserves, interest rates, and exchange rates.

Honohan (1996) notes that, driven by deregulation and innovation, the past 15 years have witnessed a sharp increase in the ratio of broad monetary aggregates (M2) to GNP—without a commensurate increase in bank capital; that is, bank leverage has increased.[19] Calvo and Goldstein (1996) argue that the same forces have made it easier for residents of emerging economies to alter the currency composition of their bank deposits whenever they get nervous about potential exchange rate changes.[20] Rojas-Suarez and Weisbrod (1995) show that banks in the largest industrial countries, when compared to their developing-country counterparts, have access to longer-term funding (on the liability side) and receive greater assistance from securities markets in spreading risks (on the asset side). Meanwhile, the recent Mexican crisis provides a graphic illustration of the risks banks face when there are large currency mismatches.[21] Between December 1993 and December 1994, the Mexican peso dropped from 3.1 to 5.3 to the dollar and the foreign-currency denominated liabilities of Mexican banks increased from 89 billion pesos to 174 billion pesos (BIS 1996); the December 1994 peso devaluation likewise resulted in a sharp fall in net worth for the business customers of Mexican banks (Mishkin 1996). Some countries have purchased extra protection against such liquid-

---

18. BIS (1996) finds that the volatility of equity prices has been much greater over the past decade in emerging countries than in large European industrial countries. Kaminsky and Reinhart (1995) report that large equity price declines have been good leading indicators of banking crises in emerging economies. See Caprio, Atiyas, and Hanson (1994) and Goldstein et al. (1993) on the bursting of property price bubbles during banking crises.

19. Using a sample of 59 developing countries, Honohan (1996) calculates that for 1980-93, the ratio of M2 to GNP has gone from 28 to 35 percent in unweighted terms and from 32 to 48 percent in weighted terms.

20. Calvo and Goldstein (1996) also show that the gap between the banking system's liquid liabilities and the stock of international reserves was much higher in Mexico just prior to the crisis than in several other Latin American emerging economies.

21. See Sheng (1996) on how in 1980 a large net foreign liability exposure subjected developing countries to large revaluation losses from subsequent devaluations under structural adjustment programs.

ity and currency mismatches by keeping banks' reserve requirements high during noncrisis times and/or by holding a relatively large stock of international reserves—but this has been the exception more than the rule. *Inadequate preparation for financial liberalization also has taken a toll* (e.g., Brazil, Chile, Finland, Indonesia, Mexico, Norway, Sweden, the United States, and Venezuela). Studies have revealed that financial liberalization is often accompanied by both rapid credit expansion (caused by pent up demand for credit and reductions in banks' reserve requirements) and high real interest rates (as banks and other financial-market participants take up new opportunities for risk taking). Credit managers and bank supervisors often do not have the expertise to deal with new credit and market risks, and, prior to liberalization, governments have frequently been reluctant to increase the training and resources devoted to bank supervision. Kaminsky and Reinhart (1995) report that the financial sector had been liberalized some time during the previous five years in 18 of the 25 banking crises in their sample.

The rap here is not against financial liberalization per se, which is widely acknowledged to offer substantial long-term benefits to emerging economies; it is instead a caveat about the risks involved if financial liberalization is not implemented in an appropriate way, that is, if it is not *preceded* by a strengthening of banking supervision.

Heavy government involvement in the banking sector and/or loose controls on connected lending also have been at the root of many developing-country banking crises, as the political objectives of governments or the personal interests of bank insiders come to supersede the commercial, profit-maximizing objectives of banks.

While privatization of state-owned banks has been on the rise, state-owned banks still account for a dominant share of banking assets in many emerging economies (see table 2.5). State-owned banks have often served as a vehicle for channeling government assistance to ailing industries. Governments often prefer this channel because it does not show up in traditional measures of the fiscal stance (e.g., the nonfinancial public-sector borrowing requirement); since they are "off-budget," such operations are more easily shielded from public scrutiny.[22] All too often, state-owned banks lack the incentive to maintain strict standards of credit quality, to identify problem loans at an early stage, to innovate, and to control costs. Loan-loss experience is typically much worse than that of privately owned banks. By the end of 1994, one-third of all loans were nonperforming in Argentina's public banks—more than three times as much as in private banks. Nonperforming loans have likewise been particularly heavy in state- or provincial-owned banks in Brazil, China, India,

---

22. See Mackenzie and Stella (1996) for a comprehensive analysis of the quasi-fiscal operations of public financial institutions.

Table 2.5 State-owned banks: percentage share of banking assets, 1994

Country	Percentage share
Hong Kong	0
India	87[a]
Indonesia	48
Korea	13
Malaysia	8
Singapore	0
Taiwan	57
Thailand	7
Argentina	36[b]
Brazil	48
Chile	14
Colombia	23
Mexico	28
Venezuela	30
Germany	50[c]
Japan	0
United States	0

a. Data refer to 1993.
b. Data refer to June 1996.
c. Not strictly comparable.

Source: IBCA Ltd., central banks, and Goldstein and Turner (1996).

and Indonesia. Even when banks are privately owned, however, efforts by governments to turn banks into their quasi-fiscal agents—by, inter alia, influencing the allocation of credit to particular sectors and industries, requiring banks to lend or to hold government bonds at below market interest rates, preventing private banks from engaging in certain profitable activities, and directing banks to borrow abroad and assume excessive currency risks—have often undermined banks' viability (BIS 1996; Caprio and Klingebiel 1996a, 1996b; Folkerts-Landau et al. 1995; Honohan 1996; Lindgren, Garcia, and Saal 1996; Mackenzie and Stella 1996; Rojas-Suarez and Weisbrod 1996b). For example, 10 years after banks were privatized in Korea, policy loans accounted for almost half of commercial bank loans (Nam 1993).

Connected lending (i.e., loans extended to bank owners and managers or their related businesses) compromises objectivity in credit assessment and produces undue concentration of credit risk. In some developing countries, connected lending is closely linked with high concentration of wealth (Rojas-Suarez and Weisbrod 1996d). Sheng (1996) and Lindgren, Garcia, and Saal (1996) cite connected lending as an important contributory factor to past banking problems in Argentina, Bangladesh, Brazil, Chile, Indonesia, Malaysia, and Thailand. Folkerts-Landau et al. (1995)

also argue that bank supervisors in developing countries have been handicapped in their efforts to monitor connected lending by borrowers' use of dummy accounts and fictitious names and by bank examiners' lack of authority to trace the use of funds.

Weaknesses in the accounting, disclosure, and legal framework are another culprit. In many developing countries, accounting conventions are not rigorous enough to prevent banks and their borrowers from concealing the true size of the nonperforming loan portfolio. Often, bad loans are made to look good by additional lending to troubled borrowers (so-called evergreening of bad loans). If loan classification is dependent only on the loan's payment status—without regard to the borrower's creditworthiness or to the market value of collateral—then the potential delay in recognizing bad loans can be considerable (De Juan 1996). And if nonperforming loans are systematically understated, loan-loss provisions are apt to be too low, and bank net income and capital will be systematically overstated (Sheng 1996; Dziobek, Frecaut, and Nieto 1995). Without accurate information on the true financial condition of banks, it is difficult for private investors and bank supervisors to monitor and discipline errant banks.

Gavin and Hausman (1996a) show that publicly reported figures on nonperforming loans gave little hint of banking crises in Chile and Colombia in the early 1980s.[23] Folkerts-Landau et al. (1995) note that in some developing countries of the Asia Pacific Economic Cooperation (APEC) forum, a loan is classified as nonperforming only after it has been in arrears for at least six months, and, in some cases, it was bank managers—not bank supervisors—that set the classification criteria. Rojas-Suarez and Weisbrod (1996d, 8), evaluating accounting and supervisory practices in Latin America, conclude that ". . . the most common failing is to provide adequate classification procedures for loan risk, resulting in underprovisioning of loans." Sheng (1996) cites one South Asian country that, until recently, allowed loans that had not been serviced for more than three years to be treated as performing. Mexican banks' planned transition to international accounting standards is expected to double the amount of past-due loans reported.

Once problem loans are identified, adequate loan-loss provisions must be established. But studies suggest that guidelines in many developing countries are unclear, weak, or altogether absent. For example, Lindgren, Josefsson, and van der Vossen (1995) reported that as of August 1995, a group of transition economies (Armenia, Azerbaijan, Georgia, Tajikistan, and Ukraine) did not have regulations obliging banks to make provisions for problem loans. Where there are such guidelines, there appears to be wide variation in coverage across countries. Table 2.6, from Goldstein and Turner (1996), presents provisioning-coverage ratios (i.e., the ratio of

---

23. See also Rojas-Suarez and Weisbrod (1996c).

Table 2.6 Provisioning coverage for nonperforming loans

Country	Loan loss reserves[a] (A) (percentage of total loans)	Nonperforming loans[b] (B) (percentage of total loans)	Coverage ratio (A/B)
Hong Kong	2.2[b]	3.1	0.7
India	–	19.5[c]	–
Indonesia	2.6	11.2	0.2
Korea	1.5	1.0	1.5
Malaysia	9.6	8.2	1.2
Singapore	–	–	1.2
Taiwan	1.1	2.6	0.4
Thailand	1.7	7.6	0.2
Argentina	10.2[b]	10.5	1.0
Brazil	1.6	5.9	0.3
Chile	3.5	1.0	3.5
Colombia	1.9	2.5	0.8
Mexico	3.1[d]	14.8	0.2
Venezuela	7.0	17.7	0.4
Japan	1.0	3.3	0.3
United States	2.7	1.6	1.7

Note: These figures may not be strictly comparable.
a. Average 1990–94.
b. Average 1994–95.
c. Relates only to public sector banks.
d. Average 1992–94.

Sources: Office of the Comptroller of the Currency, IBCA Ltd., central banks, and Goldstein and Turner (1996).

loan-loss reserves to nonperforming loans) for a sample of developing countries in the early 1990s. On average, the developing countries with the highest share of nonperforming loans tend to be the ones with the lowest provisioning coverage ratios, although there are a few exceptions (e.g., Argentina and Malaysia) where coverage in the face of a high nonperforming loan share is quite conservative.

On the disclosure side, failure to present financial and prudential information on a globally consolidated basis, differences in accounting standards across countries, lack of uniform domestic reporting requirements for banks, and an absence of serious penalties for submitting or publishing inaccurate information have often thwarted efforts by market participants to distinguish weak from strong banks (Krivoy 1996; Padoa-Schioppa 1996; Folkerts-Landau et al. 1995). While private credit-rating agencies have expanded significantly their operations in developing countries over the past decade, their coverage of banks is still much more limited than in industrial countries. Typically, large banks are rated by three of the largest such rating agencies (International Bank Credit Analyst [IBCA], Moody's Investor Service, and Standard and Poors) in only about 25 to 30 developing countries.

Legal constraints on the ability of banks to seize or transfer loan collateral, on the prompt resolution of bankruptcy cases, and on the statutory authority of bank supervisors to carry out their mandate, have increased banks' credit losses and reduced the effectiveness of supervisors in reining in excessive risk taking.[24]

A system of incentives that does not give bank owners, managers, and creditors "enough to lose" if they bring a bank to insolvency and does not give tax payers and/or bank supervisors enough institutional protection against strong pressures for regulatory forbearance has played an important role as well.

Bank capital is intended to act not only as a cushion against losses but also as an incentive for bank owners to refrain from excessive risk taking. That is, appropriate capital standards supposedly make bank owners have enough of their own money at stake to temper high-risk gambles; when capital is low, the downside risk will be disproportionately borne by the public safety net. As shown later in this chapter, bank capital in most emerging economies does not appear to be commensurate with the risks facing those economies. In addition, as highlighted by Rojas-Suarez and Weisbrod (1996d), in those developing countries with high levels of connected lending, bank owners may rather easily sidestep the intent of capital requirements by borrowing for their equity contribution from either their own bank or from the bank of a related party.[25] Where this occurs, bank owners will have no net exposure in the bank and therefore will not be restrained by fear of losing their own funds. Working in the same direction, bank restructuring programs in some developing countries have failed to penalize shareholders.[26] Again, this distorts incentives because those who would receive the lion's share of the rewards of a successful high risk investment do not symmetrically bear the lion's share of unsuccessful outcomes.

If bank managers exercise poor oversight and/or engage in imprudent behavior that leads to the insolvency of a bank, a nontrivial penalty— ranging from reduced pay or termination of employment to legal action—

---

24. Rojas-Suarez and Weisbrod (1996c) note that in Mexico the legal prohibition on using inventory as collateral for short-term business loans means that borrowers wind up paying the higher unsecured rate for these loans. Folkerts-Landau et al. (1995) emphasize that bank supervisors must have the legal authority to issue "cease and desist" orders and/or to close an insolvent bank if the supervisors' mandate is to have any credibility.

25. Consistent with this argument, Rojas-Suarez and Weisbrod (1996d) illustrate that bank owners in Latin American countries have been able to raise large amounts of capital relative to their capital base over short periods of time; in contrast, growth rates of bank capital in the larger industrial countries tend to be much lower.

26. See Rojas-Suarez and Weisbrod (1996a).

should be imposed to discourage such behavior in the future. In some developing-country cases, such penalties have been absent.[27]

Another obstacle to market discipline is the widespread practice of bailing-out bank creditors during episodes of strain or insolvency. The problem lies less with de jure deposit insurance (which is either absent or provides only partial coverage in most developing countries) than with de facto government financial assistance to protect uninsured creditors of banks.[28] Such intervention may be motivated by systemic concerns (e.g., a bank that is deemed "too large to fail") or by other perceived adverse consequences of bank failures. Meltzer (1995), for example, cites the bail-out of branches of foreign banks in Uruguay in the 1980s after their parents made such a rescue a condition for renewing loans. If the official safety net assumes a good part of the downside risk associated with lending to banks, creditors will have much less incentive to monitor bank soundness and differentiate weak from strong banks.

If anything, political pressures for regulatory forbearance are apt to be stronger in developing countries than in industrial ones. As noted earlier, developing-country banks have a dominant role in financial intermedia-tion and are well connected politically, the government is often heavily involved in the banking system, and there is less of a tradition of bank supervisor independence.[29] Also, as in industrial countries, recognition of problems at a bank can subject the supervisor to intense criticism—justified or otherwise—since the supervisor may be blamed for allowing the problem to develop. Yet the longer corrective actions or bank closure is delayed, the greater the risk that weakly capitalized or insolvent banks "gamble for resurrection." Bank supervisors end up increasing the ulti-mate taxpayer bill by delaying closure.[30]

---

27. Caprio and Klingebiel (1996b) find that bank managers were replaced in the majority of bank restructuring cases in their sample, but there were some prominent examples (e.g., Hungary in the 1990s) of senior managers merely being reassigned to other posts.

28. Padoa-Schioppa (1996), citing a Basle Committee survey, reports that of the 70 countries that at present have no formal deposit insurance coverage, all but one are developing countries; also, Lindgren, Garcia, and Saal (1996) show that most developing countries offer partial coverage in their deposit insurance arrangements, usually for retail depositors.

29. In analyzing official safety nets in Latin America, Garber (1996, 10) summarizes the political pressures facing bank supervisors as follows: "Closing down or stringently disci-plining a bank is inherently a political act in all countries. It is relatively easy to close a small bank; to close a large bank requires much more assent from the political authorities. Political authorities tend to avoid closures and overregulation of banks because they rely on the banks, first to undertake investment projects that are politically beneficial to them and second, to use the banks as funding mechanisms for their own activities. The banks can be used as a means of providing unappropriated expenditures to a particular region or sector from the fiscal authority."

30. In discussing the lessons of the US saving and loan crisis, Seidman (1996, 12) concludes that "... insolvent banks require government action, tailored to fit the individual situation,

In addition to prudential banking regulations, there are various mechanisms and institutional arrangements to reduce or offset the "moral hazard" aspects of the official safety net and the penchant to grant regulatory forbearance. These include risk-weighted deposit insurance premiums and "narrow bank" proposals that further limit the assets and permissible activities of banks receiving official safety net protection. Also relevant are depositor preference laws that put uninsured creditors—including sellers of interbank funds—at the back of the line (behind insured depositors and the deposit insurance fund) in case of bank insolvency. Finally, there are rule-based supervisory regimes that try to mimic (via government-directed corrective actions) the pressures the private market would impose on errant banks if there were no official safety net, prescribe bank closure while the bank still has positive net worth, require greater public accountability from senior policymakers that invoke "too large to fail" emergency financial assistance, and require bank supervisors to implement "prompt corrective action" once bank capital falls below specified multiple capital-zone trip wires.[31] However, such incentive-compatible institutional arrangements have rarely been present and operative in developing countries. (They have been the exception in industrial countries as well.)

Poor information systems on the creditworthiness of bank customers, along with its adverse consequences for the quality of the credit review process, have also been a serious handicap.

Kane (1995) has highlighted the constraints that poor information systems have placed on efforts by developing-country banks to exercise due diligence in making new loans and monitoring outstanding ones. Kane notes that evaluation of the creditworthiness of would-be borrowers is hampered by the fact that data on the traditional "five Cs" of creditworthiness—cash flow, capital, collateral, character, and conditional economic vulnerability—are often lacking. Computer software routinely used by banks in industrial countries for credit scoring and tracking the changing probability of default after making a loan is not yet in use in most developing countries. In addition, Kane points out that private credit bureaus and rating agencies—which could help fill these information gaps—are just beginning to set up or expand operations in many developing countries.

---

and the longer the corrective action is delayed the more costly and destabilized the problems will be."

31. Several of these mechanisms were incorporated in US banking reform as part of the 1991 Federal Deposit Insurance Corporation Improvement Act (FDICIA)—see Benston and Kaufman (1996) and chapter 3 of this study. See Litan (1987) for the argument in support of "narrow banks." Yet another mechanism for resisting pressures for regulatory forbearance is to house banking supervision in a relatively autonomous government agency.

In many developing countries, these weaknesses in the credit review process are compounded by failures on the part of bank supervisors to evaluate rigorously the credit analysis performed by banks. De Juan (1996) has argued that high quality on-site inspection of the loan portfolio is essential because bank reports are unreliable when banks are in trouble; to perform this on-site inspection properly, supervisors need direct access to individual borrowers' files. De Juan (1996) blames Spanish bank examiners' lack of on-site examination skills in the late 1970s and early 1980s for the failure to discover insolvencies until very late in the game.

Finally, *the exchange rate regime has sometimes complicated crisis prevention and management efforts*—either because a long overvalued fixed exchange rate has invited speculative attack against the currency (and brought increased strains on the banking system in its wake),[32] or because exchange rate commitments have limited the central bank's ability to act as lender-of-last-resort to illiquid but solvent banks. For example, Argentina's Convertibility Law put strong constraints on the responses of the Central Bank of Argentina to a large deposit withdrawal from the banking system in the immediate aftermath of the 1994-95 Mexican economic crisis; indeed, if the Argentinean authorities could not have injected liquidity by reducing relatively high reserve requirements, the banking system might have found its capacity to cope with that threat wanting (Fernandez 1996).[33]

The Adequacy of Existing International Banking Agreements

The problems in developing-country banking systems outlined above are not being addressed adequately by existing international agreements[34] on banking supervision.

Quite apart from macroeconomic and exchange rate policies (which lie outside the realm of financial supervision), many of the factors instrumental in developing-country banking crises (e.g., heavy government ownership/involvement in the banking system, poor asset classification and provisioning practices, a high degree of connected lending, weak informa-

---

32. Hausman and Gavin (1995) conclude that unsustainable exchange rate pegs have contributed more than any other factor to the relatively high volatility of GNP growth rates in Latin American developing countries over the past two decades. Kaminsky and Reinhart (1995) find that no other leading indicator of banking crises in developing countries has performed better than real exchange rate overvaluation.

33. Because of the constraints that a currency board places on the central bank's ability to act as a lender of last resort, countries with such exchange arrangements may find it useful to find other institutions (e.g., a group of international commercial banks) that can play the role during a liquidity crisis; see Williamson (1995).

34. See chapter 3 of this study for an explanation of why *international* banking agreements can sometimes overcome obstacles that *national* reform efforts cannot.

tion and disclosure systems, and intense political pressures for regulatory forbearance) are simply not covered by existing international agreements. Perhaps the Basle Committee on Banking Supervision did not see some of these problems as so pressing in the G-10 countries. Or maybe differences in practices and/or attitudes on some issues (e.g., asset classification and provisioning rules, closure procedures for failed banks, the mix between discretion and rules in bank supervision) were too wide even among the G-10 to merit pursuit of an international guideline. Perhaps the judgment was made that even if agreement could be reached, a more comprehensive international banking standard would be too intrusive or costly to implement. Or maybe the G-10 composition of the Basle Committee just made it less attuned more generally to the banking problems of developing countries. Whatever the explanation, the current situation is that developing countries who are looking for international guidelines on which to model their own banking reform efforts have thus far had relatively little to latch on to. As the chairman of the Basle Committee, Padoa-Schioppa, recently acknowledged (Padoa-Schioppa 1996, 13):

> For such (emerging market) countries, the Basle rules may not provide sufficient support to the fulfillment of the basic prerequisites for sound banking, or be too sophisticated and difficult to comply with, or disregard specific problems that are not acute in G-10 economies. Where capital and markets are thin, or competition among banks is not working properly, supervisors may well need to interfere more deeply with the operation of the market.

In a similar vein, W. White (1996, 32) concludes:

> . . . market discipline in developing countries might be enhanced by having some international agreement as to what constitutes prudent behavior. At the moment, there is no such agreement.

When specific banking problems have been addressed by international agreement (e.g., inadequate bank capital, lack of effective consolidated supervision by home supervisors, weak cooperation between home and host-country supervisors), questions have arisen about whether the particular circumstances of developing countries have been taken adequately into account and about the degree of developing-country implementation of those agreements.

Consider the 1988 Basle Capital Adequacy Accord for credit risk.[35] This accord sets minimum capital requirements for internationally active banks. More specifically, it assigns different risk weights to various categories of bank assets (including off-balance-sheet items), defines elements to be counted as bank capital, and establishes ratio requirements of 4

---

35. The Basle Capital Adequacy Accord was amended in December 1995 to include market risk (Basle Committee on Banking Supervision 1996; IMF 1995).

Table 2.7a Basle capital adequacy accord: risk weights

Assets included	Risk category	Risk weight (percent)
Balance sheet items:		
Cash and loans to governments and central banks	1	0
Claims on public sector entities	2	10
Claims on OECD banks	3	20
Loans secured by mortgages on residential property	4	50
All other assets, including commercial loans	5	100
Off-balance-sheet items:		
Each off-balance-sheet item is scaled by a conversion factor	6	Applicable weight

Table 2.7b Basle capital adequacy accord: tier 1 and tier 2 capital

Capital measure	Components	Recommended ratio
Tier 1	Paid-up capital (common stock) and disclosed reserves.	At least 4 percent.
Tier 2	Undisclosed, revaluation, and general loan-loss reserves; subordinated debt; and hybrid debt instruments.	Limited to 100 percent of tier 1 capital.
Total	Tier 1 plus tier 2 (where tier 1 can range from 50 percent to 100 percent of the total).	At least 8 percent of which at least 4 percent is tier 1 capital.

Source: Lindgren, Garcia, and Saal (1996).

percent of risk-weighted assets for tier 1 capital and 8 percent for total capital (tier 1 plus tier 2 capital). Table 2.7 summarizes key features of the accord.

From the perspective of developing countries, the Basle Capital Adequacy Accord has been criticized on two grounds: first, it does not provide an incentive for banks operating in countries with more volatile environments to hold higher capital, and second, the significance of meeting the minimum capital ratio is reduced if other elements of the prudential/supervisory framework are substandard.

For many developing countries, average volatilities for the variables relevant to credit risk can be two or three times higher (if not more) than those in industrial countries (Hausman and Gavin 1995; Goldstein and Turner 1996). Reflecting, inter alia, this empirical regularity, virtually all analysts conclude that banks in most developing countries should be holding much higher capital than those in industrial countries (Gavin and Hausman 1996a; Goldstein and Turner 1996; Kane 1995; Krivoy 1996).[36] Yet, the accord applies the same risk weight to a commercial loan in Venezuela as it does in the United States. Similarly, the accord assigns the same risk weight to a Brazilian bank's holding of local-currency-denominated and -funded Brazilian government bonds as it does to a Dutch bank's holding of Dutch government bonds (even though the default history is quite different).[37] The point is that (ex ante) default rates between industrial and developing countries within a given Basle risk-weight class (say, for commercial loans) may differ by more than default rates across risk-weight classes (say, between home mortgage loans and commercial loans) within a developing country. That is, what the risk-weighting process does not consider may be more important for developing-country banks than what it does consider.[38]

Implicit in the Basle Accord is the assumption that there is appropriate provisioning for bad loans. Where that is the case, bad loans can be written off without reducing the bank's capital, that is, bank capital will be tapped only when major unforeseen loan problems arise. As noted earlier, however, there are many developing countries where loan-loss provisioning rules and practices are weak. In such an environment, bank capital provides a much smaller cushion of safety than when provisioning is adequate. (That is, the second line of defense against credit losses is more vulnerable if the first line of defense is porous.) This has led Dziobek, Frecaut, and Nieto (1995, 13) to conclude:

> Applying the Basle 8 percent rule without adequate provisioning distorts the informational value of the capital ratio. Worse than that, compliance with the 8

36. Kaufman (1996a, 11) offers the following conclusion: "The 8 percent risk-based capital standard was developed for major banks in industrialized countries. . . . The standards were not meant for other countries. Nevertheless, they have been 'borrowed' by other countries that have much greater macroeconomic stability, narrower financial markets, and less effective supervision. As a result, the 8 percent standard is far too low for most, if not all, of these countries. Moreover, the risk weights applied to the assets are even less appropriate than they are for the developed countries . . ."

37. Assigning a low risk weight to bank holdings of government debt in developing counties has also been criticized for facilitating governments' implicit and off-budget taxation of the banking system (Krivoy 1996). By making holding of government bonds (often at below market interest rates) more attractive for meeting bank capital requirements, the government finds it easier to finance budget deficits. Dziobek, Frecaut, and Nieto (1995) also argue that the 20 percent risk weight on interbank loans is inappropriate (too low) for developing countries because the liquidity of the market and quality of information on counterparts are typically much below those in industrial countries.

38. The accord does take some recognition of sovereign risk by placing a higher risk weight on bank loans to foreign governments that are not members of the Organization for Economic Cooperation and Development (OECD) or do not subscribe to the IMF General Agreement to Borrow. In this sense, the accord provides incentives for developing-country banks to hold higher capital against loans to other developing countries but not against loans made domestically.

Table 2.8 Required and actual bank capital ratios (percentages), 1995

Country	Capital adequacy ratio (national requirements)	Actual risk-based capital ratio
Hong Kong	8[a]	17.5[b]
India	8	9.5[c]
Indonesia	8	11.9
Korea, South	8	9.3
Malaysia	8	11.3
Singapore	12[d]	18.7[d]
Taiwan	8	12.2
Thailand	8	9.3
Argentina	12	18.5
Brazil	8[e]	12.9
Chile	8[f]	10.7
Colombia	9	13.5
Mexico	8	11.3
Israel	8	10.5[g]
South Africa	8[h]	10.1
Japan	8	9.1
United States	8	12.8

Notes: Several European countries have significantly higher capital ratios. Definitions sometimes differ from those applied by the Basle Committee.

a. 12 percent for some banks, and 16 percent for some nonbanks.
b. Relates to locally incorporated authorized institutions and is on a consolidated basis.
c. Relates only to public-sector banks.
d. Based only on Tier 1 capital.
e. Plus 1.5 percent on national value of swap operations.
f. Legislation now before Congress.
g. 1994.
h. Higher ratios for some banks.

Source: Goldstein and Turner (1996).

percent capital rule without adequate reserves for loans of doubtful quality renders the ratio meaningless as banks may boost capital ratios at the expense of provisioning.

Following a similar line of reasoning, several other analysts have argued that high levels of connected lending (Rojas-Suarez and Weisbrod 1996d) or weaknesses in other elements of the financial infrastructure (Kane 1995) make the 8 percent capital rule less indicative of bank safety in developing countries than in industrial ones.

In defense of the accord, it could be argued that by specifying the Basle risk-weighted standard as a minimum, sufficient flexibility was already built-in to accommodate those countries that face higher than average risks. They would merely need to compensate for that higher risk by holding higher capital than the minimum. Table 2.8 shows that this expectation has generally *not* been met. With several notable exceptions (e.g., Argentina, Colombia, Hong Kong, and Singapore), developing-country governments have not set national capital standards much above the Basle minimum, and their banks have not held actual capital much above that for banks in countries with significantly more stable operating environments.

Another relevant example of weaknesses in existing international banking agreements is the Basle Committee's 1992 Minimum Standards paper. This paper laid out four principles designed to ensure effective supervision of international banks and good cooperation between home- and host-country authorities (BIS 1996; W. White 1996). One of those principles allows the host country to impose restrictive measures or prohibit the establishment of banking offices if it determines that the home country is not exercising effective consolidated supervision. However, as noted in a recent Basle Committee on Banking Supervision report (1996), host supervisors have no common standard to judge what constitutes effective consolidated supervision by home supervisors. In addition, implementation has proved difficult. Four years after the launch, 20 percent of those countries responding to a Basle Committee survey indicated that they do not yet consolidate financial and prudential information on banks' global operations (Padoa-Schioppa 1996); the remaining 80 percent reported that they still face difficulties in verifying the reliability of such data through on-site inspections, and almost one-fifth of the respondents admitted that they still do not make approval of the home-country authority a condition for the establishment of a foreign bank. This has led the chairman of the Basle Committee, Padoa-Schioppa, to offer the appraisal that the implementation of the minimum standards is proceeding too slowly (Padoa-Schioppa 1996). It also raises the question of whether compliance incentives are strong enough.

Despite these limitations, I do not share the view that existing international agreements on banking supervision have been of no value to developing countries. In the absence of those agreements, effective capital ratios in developing-country banks probably would have been even lower, there would have been a lower degree of cooperation between banking supervisors in those countries and their counterparts in the industrial countries, and there may well have been an even higher incidence of banking crises in developing countries than actually occurred.

Alternative Approaches to Banking and Supervisory Reform in Developing Countries

How can we improve on the existing international banking agreements we already have, with emphasis on quickly bringing more developing countries up to a minimum level of sound banking practice and strong banking supervision?

One approach would be to stand pat with existing international agreements and accept (if only grudgingly) the proposition that the threshold motivation needed for serious banking reform may only occur after a banking crisis. To be sure, there have been cases (e.g., Argentina, Chile, Hong Kong, and the United States) where banking crises were followed by the adoption of an improved incentive and/or supervisory framework. The disadvantages here are twofold:

- because banking crises are so costly, approaches that can motivate reform *before* a crisis takes place should be favored, and

- most banking crises are *not* followed by significant banking reform.

On the latter, Caprio and Klingebiel (1996b) studied 64 episodes of bank restructuring, involving 55 developing countries. Four criteria (financial deepening, development of real credit, real deposit interest rates, and recurrent problems in the banking system after restructuring) were used to evaluate these restructuring exercises. Only Chile and Malaysia were judged to be clear successes.[39] Twenty-four restructuring exercises achieved mixed success, and 27 were evaluated as either unsuccessful or not yet resolved.

A second approach would count on expanded bilateral and multilateral technical assistance cum market discipline. The difficulty here is that technical assistance, helpful though it is, will not likely overcome the domestic political resistance to reform. That is, poor banking supervision is not simply a matter of knowing how to do it; it is also a matter of overcoming the political resistance to doing the right thing. Market discipline can be a powerful incentive for errant banks to get their house in order. But experience suggests that market discipline does not operate effectively where there is little/poor publicly available information on the creditworthiness of a borrower or a strong expectation that the public sector will bailout a troubled borrower. As indicated above, the quantity and quality of publicly available information on banks and on their customers are still significantly poorer in developing countries than in the industrial world. In addition, incentives for banks to leverage risk on the official safety net are probably even more pervasive in developing countries than in industrial ones. Calomiris (1996), for example, recounts the tales of Chile during the 1980s and Venezuela during the early 1990s, where political will to limit safety net protection melted away in the heat

---

39. Caprio and Klingebiel (1996b) regard the bank restructuring exercise as a clear success if the country receives good performance on all four criteria. Good performance on two to three criteria elicits a grade of mixed results, and a score of zero or one puts the country into the unsuccessful or not yet resolved category.

of bank adversity.[40] Even in the United States, the empirical literature has found it difficult to identify a reliable link between measures of the riskiness of bank assets and interest rate spreads on banks' subordinated debt (Avery, Belton, and Goldberg 1988; Gorton and Santomero 1990).[41] An expanded role for market discipline in many developing countries therefore awaits prior or simultaneous progress on disclosure and on limiting public-sector bailouts. In short, while technical assistance and market discipline are an important part of the banking reform package, they cannot be the whole package.

A third tack would be to rely on host countries where developing-country banks want to do business. As noted, the Basle Committee's Minimum Standards, as well as some national banking legislation (e.g., the United States), permits the host country, inter alia, to prohibit foreign banking offices within its borders if it is not satisfied that the home country is implementing effective supervision. This too carries a good deal of potential leverage, at least for banks whose business strategies would be seriously damaged by exclusion from certain large foreign markets. But actual leverage is apt to be much lower. If countries that already have banking offices in the host country are grandfathered, only new entrants will be affected. And concerns about misuse of such a policy for protectionist purposes are likely to constrain its use only to the most flagrant cases of weak supervision. In addition, as noted by Rodrik (1995), it has become much less politically acceptable for one country to try to impose conditionality on another.

This brings us to the fourth approach, namely, the setting and monitoring of an IBS. Such an IBS would go beyond existing international agreements in an attempt to tackle more of the factors underlying banking crises in developing countries.[42] Although a bank's participation in an IBS would be voluntary, market participants' knowledge of who is or is not meeting the standard would establish market penalties for slow movers. Peer pressures should also operate in the desired direction. Other incentives for signing on to an IBS might be offered by the official sector

---

40. It is because of these two shortcomings that I remain skeptical that a proposal to require banks to hold a certain percentage of capital as subordinated debt (Calomiris 1996) could, at this stage, serve as the centerpiece of market discipline for banks in most developing countries.

41. Flannery and Sorescu (1996) have more success at finding a link between subordinated debt prices and banks' default risks. They note, however, that such a relationship was stronger in some periods (1989-91, when conjectural guarantees no longer covered many bank debentures) than during others (1983-90). In addition, Flannery and Sorescu (1996, 1374) conclude that "our results provide no indication that market discipline could (or could not) entirely replace government supervision of bank risk taking."

42. Early support for an IBS can be found in Goldstein (1996a, 1996b).

to reward crisis prevention measures.[43] For example, the terms at which countries gain access to international lender-of-last resort facilities (e.g., the IMF's New Agreement to Borrow or access limits under the IMF's general resources) could depend in part on IBS participation; similarly, the risk weights in the Basle capital standard might be made more favorable for IBS signatories.

A cue might be taken from recent efforts by the public and private sectors to strengthen other elements of the international supervisory and regulatory regime.[44]

Perhaps the most significant recent official-sector initiative is the IMF's Special Data Dissemination Standard (SDDS), established in April 1996 following lapses in the publication of economic and financial data prior to the Mexican crisis. Countries subscribing to the SDDS agree to meet specific requirements with respect to coverage, periodicity, and timeliness of economic and financial data, public access to these data, and the integrity and quality of the data (see appendix B). Also, the IMF is to maintain an electronic bulletin board that will list the countries subscribing to the standard, along with relevant explanatory material about the data series. Countries on the list subscribe to, and intend to meet, certain tenets of good statistical citizenship; serious and persistent nonobservance is cause for removal. As of February 1997, 42 countries (including 18 developing countries) had subscribed to the SDDS (see appendix B, table B.1).

In a similar vein, a consensus developed in the late 1980s that existing standards and practices for clearance and settlement in the world's securities markets were deficient and uneven across countries, with adverse effects for international investment flows and management of systemic risk. It was agreed that global market infrastructure could be improved if countries had a set of international benchmarks/standards against which they could evaluate their own clearance and settlements systems, along with a target date for implementation. This time it was a private-sector organization, the Group of Thirty (G-30), that took the lead in laying out these best-practice guidelines; the guidelines were then updated in 1995 by the International Society of Securities Administrators (ISSA).[45] Appendix B summarizes the original G-30 recommendations on

---

43. The principle here is the same as that commonly applied to the purchase of insurance. If you are a smoker and very overweight, you can still get life insurance, but you will pay more for it than if you take measures to reduce your risk.

44. Ongoing efforts to agree on an investment code for OECD countries, harmonize payments systems within the European Union, and discourage corruption via an international agreement on tax deductibility provide examples of using international or regional standards to overcome national inertia in dealing with commonly perceived problems. The International Organization of Securities Commissions (IOSCO) also is currently at work on a set of guidelines for international securities markets.

45. See World Bank (1997) for a description of the ISSA revised guidelines for clearance and settlement.

clearance and settlement. According to a recent World Bank (1997) report, emerging markets had made major strides in meeting many of the G-30 standards (see appendix B, table B.3).

A similar exercise, again spearheaded by the G-30 (1993), took place in the early 1990s when rapid growth of derivative markets raised concerns that dealers and users of these products had not established appropriate risk-management systems.[46] Appendix B summarizes the G-30 recommendation in this area. Approximately a year after launch, a follow-up survey suggested that from 20 to 50 percent of market participants implemented the various recommendations (G-30 1994; IMF 1995).

Last but not least, the Basle Committee's 1988 Capital Adequacy Accord was a direct response to a need for both a better safety cushion for internationally active banks and a more level playing field. Warts and all, the 1988 accord has probably induced internationally active banks to be better capitalized and has focused greater attention on the riskiness of bank assets. By 1993, all industrial countries had adopted the accord's standard (after incorporating it in national legislation), and, by now, 80-90 other countries (most of them developing countries) have either adopted the standard outright or followed a Basle-type approach in setting their national capital standards (Padoa-Schioppa 1996).

In each case, an international standard offered incentives for countries to make improvements that they might not have been able or willing to make unilaterally. Regulatory and supervisory reforms involve both costs and benefits, and coordination difficulties and asymmetric information can affect the incentives for undertaking such reforms. Increases in minimum capital adequacy standards are a good example of this incentive problem. Because equity holders are generally less protected from bank insolvencies than other creditors, they typically demand a higher rate of return than depositors or bond holders. As such, it is costly for banks to go to the market to increase their capital. Regulators' attempts to unilaterally increase minimum capital adequacy standards for national banks are likely to meet resistance because of charges that national banks will lose competitiveness to banks in other countries. But if authorities in the major financial centers agree to coordinate increases in bank capital requirements, then that opposition from national banks is apt to be much reduced (since the level playing field will be maintained).

It was apparently just such considerations that led to the 1988 Basle Capital Adequacy Accord.[47] In the aftermath of the developing-country

---

46. The original G-30 recommendations on derivatives have been followed by further guidelines, promulgated by both the official and private sectors; see IMF (1995, 1996a) for a summary of these initiatives.

47. W. White (1996, 19) offers the following observation on the 1988 Basle Capital Adequacy Accord: "Individual countries cannot regulate or supervise their domestic institutions and markets without recognizing the implications for international competitiveness. In the United

debt crisis, then-Federal Reserve Chairman Paul A. Volcker (along with other US banking regulators) was concerned that US money-center banks were undercapitalized. Also, US banks were losing business to internationally active Japanese banks—in part because the latter were subject to more lax capital requirements and lower funding costs. Volcker saw that a unilateral effort to increase capital requirements for US banks was encountering sharp domestic opposition (especially in the US Congress) because of considerations of international competitiveness. Meanwhile, the UK regulatory authorities were coming to the same diagnosis on capital, but were not happy with a bank capital proposal then being floated within the European Community.[48] The result was first (in 1987) a US-UK agreement on minimal bank capital requirements, followed soon after by a G-10 agreement (i.e., the Basle Accord). This is another example of the broader proposition that international coordination can sometimes achieve outcomes that are not available with uncoordinated policy measures (Frenkel, Goldstein, and Masson 1990).

Turning to the payoff from regulatory reforms, a country that can convince creditors that such reforms have improved banking safety and soundness may be rewarded by a lower risk premium on its obligations. However, it may be difficult for creditors to verify on their own that the borrower has really undertaken serious reform—particularly if the borrower operates primarily in unfamiliar overseas markets. "False" reformers will be tempted to claim they have reformed their banking systems so that they too can benefit from lower funding costs. If the "true" reformers cannot somehow differentiate themselves from the impostors, the former will not be able to obtain the appropriate market payoff from regulatory reform, and, hence, may be discouraged from undertaking these reforms in the first place.

One potential solution to this asymmetric information or "lemons" problem is for true reformers to join voluntarily a "club" with demanding entry conditions and international monitoring of reforms.[49] The club will then certify that its members are true reformers, enabling members to obtain the full market payoff. This rationale is often advanced to explain why borrowers might seek a credit rating from internationally recognized,

---

States, for example, efforts to force banks to hold more capital in the early 1980s (in light of the Mexican crisis) led to stiff industry resistance on competitive grounds and led directly to strengthened efforts within the Basle Committee on Banking Supervision to come up with an international agreement." Kapstein (1991) tells a similar story in his account of the history of the Basle Accord.

48. See Kapstein (1991) for a detailed account of the factors in a US-UK agreement.

49. See Mishkin (1994, 1996) for a discussion of how asymmetric information influences institutional arrangements in national and international financial markets. The "lemons problem"—which centers on how asymmetric information can prevent market prices from reflecting true quality differences—was introduced by Akerlof (1970).

private credit-rating agencies. But the same reasoning would apply to the IMF's SDDS, the G-30's guidelines, or an IBS. After all, one way to interpret a voluntary IBS is as a club for countries undertaking reforms of their banking systems and their supervisory arrangements. An IBS lends further credibility to banking reform efforts—much in the same way that IMF support lends credibility to national stabilization programs. If the geographic coverage of private credit-rating agencies continues to expand and if those firms prove adept at evaluating banks' creditworthiness, it may eventually become possible for the private sector to take over this certification process—but in the interim the best solution may be an IBS.

An IBS, with a reasonable transition period for implementation, would give those developing countries that are still in the planning stages of banking reform some concrete benchmarks and a fixed timetable to follow. For countries that were in the process of reform, it would provide a way of gauging progress. Countries whose banking systems and supervisory regimes already met or exceeded the standards would not be constrained by them and would receive assurance that their counterparts had taken measures to improve their creditworthiness. Together, these groups ought to make up a powerful constituency for an IBS.

Operational Issues Associated with an IBS

Laying out the general case for an IBS is one thing. Writing the specifics of such a standard is another. Much of the devil is in the details. In this chapter, I offer specific answers to the following key questions:

- Should the IBS be a unitary or two-level standard?
- What elements of banking and banking supervision should an IBS include?
- Who should set the standard?
- How should compliance with an IBS be monitored and encouraged?

Before addressing those specific operational issues, I will consider eight broad points about what an IBS can achieve and how it ought to be designed.

Broad Features of an IBS

First, an IBS is not a panacea. It would be unrealistic to expect an IBS to eliminate banking crises in developing countries—particularly if these countries do not make significant progress in reducing macroeconomic instability and the size and frequency of exchange rate misalignments. When the macroeconomy is in trouble and the real exchange rate is allowed to get way out of line, the banking system is sure to suffer. An IBS can improve mechanisms that cushion against macroeconomic volatility—bank capital, provisioning for loan losses, etc.—and it can reduce the independent contribution of banking-system weakness to an unhealthy macroeconomic environment. But an IBS *cannot be a substitute for disciplined monetary, fiscal, and exchange rate policies*, and it cannot engineer structural changes in the real economy (such as greater diversification in a country's export structure) to reduce volatility.[1]

Also, even in countries with the most developed systems of banking supervision, many future bank failures go undetected during bank examinations. For example, a recent Federal Deposit Insurance Corporation (FDIC) (1996) study found that of the US banks that failed from 1980 to 1994, 36 percent of them had received the highest bank examination ratings (that is, CAMEL ratings of 1 and 2) two years prior to failure.[2]

An IBS should be seen as part of a comprehensive reform effort for banking and banking supervision (that would also include increased training for bank supervisors and improvements in the broader financial and legal infrastructure). A realistic objective for an IBS is that it lead to a lower frequency of serious banking crises in developing countries than would occur in its absence; given the costs of past banking crises in developing countries, this objective—if it can be achieved—would represent an important accomplishment.

Second, if an IBS is going to make a real dent in the incidence of serious banking crises in developing countries, it will need to *encompass an interrelated set of banking system and supervisory reforms*. Changing one or two elements of the banking architecture is unlikely to make a large difference. For example:

- If nothing is done to improve accounting and provisioning practices, neither statements of a bank's financial condition nor measures of bank capital will be accurate; as such, public disclosure will not fortify market discipline, and prompt-corrective-action supervisory measures based on capital-zone tripwires will be ineffective.

- If nothing is done about connected lending, increasing capital requirements for banks will not alter the incentives for excessive risk taking by bank owners.

- If nothing is done to institute prompt corrective action by bank supervisors, there may be little consequence of bank capital—even correctly measured—dropping below the regulatory requirement.

---

1. As emphasized in chapter 2, a lack of diversification in the loan book of developing-country banks countributes to their vulnerability.

2. If one excludes types of bank failures that cannot be anticipated by safety and soundness examinations, as well as bank examinations that were more than one year old, the percentage of failed banks that had CAMEL ratings of 1 or 2 two years before failure drops to 16 percent (FDIC 1996). CAMEL is an abbreviation for five components of bank soundness: capital, assets, management, earnings, and liquidity. In an earlier study of the same issue, Benston (1973) found that of US commercial banks that failed from 1959 to 1971, almost 60 percent had been rated "no problem" on the last bank exam prior to collapse. Benston (1973) goes on to argue that the main reason examinations fail to predict bank failures is

- If nothing is done to make government policymakers more accountable for granting "too big to fail" assistance to severely undercapitalized banks, then private creditors will not heed any improved public information on banks.

- If nothing is done to reduce the proclivity of governments to use banks as their quasi-fiscal agents, efforts to improve the credit review process are apt to be frustrated.

- If nothing is done to buttress the legal authority of bank supervisors, then tougher prudential standards are not likely to be enforceable.

In other words, there is a critical mass of reforms in developing countries that, if not achieved, may result in little improvement in the bottom line.

One frequent criticism of such a comprehensive approach to banking reform is that some of these elements would go beyond the traditional jurisdiction of banking supervisors (e.g., the Basle Committee of Bank Supervisors). For example, efforts to increase the transparency of government involvement in the banking system (by, for example, including such quasi-fiscal operations in the government's budgetary figures) are more the responsibility of the IMF than of the Basle Committee. Similarly, international accounting standards fall in the sphere of the International Federation of Accountant's International Accounting Standards Committee (IASC). Facilitating bank seizure of collateral on nonperforming loans involves changes in countries' legal codes. And better preparation for financial liberalization will require, inter alia, more training of bank supervisors, which is part of ongoing activities of the World Bank and the regional development banks.

My rebuttal to the jurisdictional argument is that if serious banking reform requires a coordinated effort among bank supervisors and other interested official parties, then a vigorous effort should be made to obtain such cross-agency cooperation. If that means one official institution cannot be solely responsible for designing an IBS, so be it.[3]

Third, an IBS does not imply (full) international harmonization of banking standards. So long as an IBS is designed as a *minimum set of international banking standards*, it represents only a *partial international harmonization* of standards, that is, it still leaves room—beyond the minimum—for individual countries to maintain their national preferences toward risk, as well to maintain some of their institutional diversity.[4] For example, if Argentina wants its banks to disclose more information on their financial

---

that a leading cause of failure is fraud or misdealing, and bank examinations are not effective in detecting these kinds of problems.

3. This issue will be taken up again later in this chapter.

4. For a discussion of different levels of harmonization of international regulatory standards, see Herring and Litan (1995). For an analysis of why it is not desirable to impose the same

condition than stipulated in the IBS, it would be free to do so. Likewise, since an IBS would not step into the debate on the securities and insurance activities of banks, it would not stop France and Germany from maintaining their universal banking structures, while the United States and Japan could continue their de jure limitation on such activities by banks. An IBS that stops well short of full harmonization of banking structures and supervisory practices merits emphasis because, as illustrated in appendix C, tables C.1 and C.2, there remain significant differences on these matters even among the G-10 and EU countries.

Fourth, an IBS would not necessarily decrease competition in the banking industry. As highlighted by L. White (1996), in industries where *national* governments act to reduce competition, an *international standard can serve to reduce national protectionism*. Two examples suffice to illustrate the point. If governments provide state-owned banks with cheap capital and routinely bailout such institutions when they suffer large credit losses, an IBS that discourages these subsidies (or taxes) can increase global competition in the banking industry. Likewise, if generous national safety nets induce banks to substitute official (implicit or explicit) safety-net guarantees for private capital, then an IBS that sets a minimum international capital standard can reduce these national subsidies toward banks and increase competition (L. White 1996).

Fifth, like other international regulatory initiatives, an IBS needs to confront the test that there be *market failures, externalities (spillovers), or public goods that extend beyond national borders*, and that cannot be handled adequately by national regulation (Herring and Litan 1995; L. White 1996). As argued in chapter 2, I believe an IBS can pass that test: there are nontrivial cross-border spillover effects of developing-country banking crises; there are market failures associated with asymmetric information, with connected lending, and with heavy involvement of national governments in the banking industry; and accurate and timely public information on the financial condition of banks has attributes of a public good. Also, based on the history of the past 15 years, it is unlikely that competition among national banking regulators in developing countries will motivate serious banking reform.

Sixth, an IBS must consider the *costs of regulation and the possibility that flawed or outmoded regulations* could make matters worse. That is, there can be government failure as well as market failure. [5] It is partly for this reason that an IBS ought to be *voluntary*. If countries view the costs of participating in an IBS as higher than the benefits, they need not sign up. Similarly, if they decide that changes in the structure of the banking

---

organizational structure on financial markets in all countries, see Kaufman and Kroszner (1996).

5. See Merton (1995) for a discussion of the risks associated with implementing the wrong global regulatory standard.

industry have made an IBS outmoded or counterproductive—and agreement can not be reached on a revision of the IBS—they can withdraw. In this sense, countries will vote with their feet as to whether the IBS is a club worth joining.

Seventh, an IBS should include *both quantitative and qualitative elements*. The prescription for some regulatory and supervisory problems (e.g., minimum bank capital ratios, limits on connected lending) can and should be delineated in quantitative terms, but many other problems (improved public disclosure, prompt corrective action on the part of bank supervisors, stricter accounting and provisioning practices, etc.) are best handled primarily in qualitative terms. Indeed, appendix B shows that many of the more useful international guidelines in the financial area have been qualitative in nature. Whether quantitative or qualitative, IBS guidelines need to be *specific enough to serve as benchmarks* for performance evaluation by the monitoring agency (e.g., it will not be sufficient to call for appropriate asset classification unless some indication is given about what "appropriate" means).

Eighth, as with the IMF's SDDS, *countries* (not individual banks) *would sign on to an IBS*. Once a country agreed to participate, it would alter its national banking laws (if necessary) to accommodate any features of the IBS not already included; at that point, a country's banks would be covered.[6] But what about banks in a country that chose not to participate in the IBS? In that case, individual banks wanting to distinguish themselves from their less creditworthy competitors could indicate that they voluntarily comply with all elements of an IBS under their control (much in the same way that some derivative dealers advertise that they voluntarily implement the G-30 guidelines on risk management of derivatives). Admittedly, they could not claim that national supervisory practices were subject to international monitoring, but they still might get some market premium by subscribing to a higher code of conduct.

A Unitary or Two-Level Standard?

An IBS could be a unitary standard applicable to all countries, or alternatively, a two-level standard where countries themselves would decide at which level to join. All previous international banking agreements have

---

6. Should all banks be covered or only internationally active banks? The Basle Capital Adequacy Accord, for example, was directed only at the latter group. The rationale for covering only internationally active banks is that these banks generate the largest international spillovers. The argument for wider coverage is that widespread failures at domestic banks generate (smaller but still) nontrivial spillover effects; domestically oriented banks represent too large a share of vulnerability to ignore; and, as developing countries increase their financial links with the rest of the world, more of their banks will become internationally active. I would argue for the wider definition of participating banks.

been unitary standards. It is argued that a unitary standard ensures all countries receive uniform treatment; it is also easier to administer.

Despite these considerations, I vote for a two-level standard on three grounds: differences in country circumstances, relevant transition periods, and lessons from standards in other areas. Moreover, potential difficulties with a two-level mandatory standard are reduced when the IBS is voluntary instead.

Some of the most widespread and severe banking problems are among the transition economies and developing countries of Africa and Asia. Yet financial and banking structures and the degree of market orientation in these countries are typically quite different from those in the more advanced emerging economies. What is of first priority and feasible in the way of banking reform is therefore likely to be different in say, China, Russia, and India than in say, Hong Kong and Chile. For example, the share of total banking assets owned by the state is almost 90 percent in India, whereas it is zero in both Hong Kong and Singapore. A two-level standard would better accommodate these differences.

A two-level standard would lead to a more desirable transition period than would a unitary one. Note that implementation of the Basle Accord on risk-weighted capital standards took four years for the G-10 countries; similarly, as noted earlier, implementation of the Minimum Standards guidelines has been incomplete and uneven across countries four years after its agreement. The IMF's SDDS, applicable only to countries heavily involved in international capital markets, will have a transition period of two and one-half years. If there is a unitary standard, then a choice must be made between setting it at a high level (i.e., "best practice" guidelines) or a low level (i.e., a minimum standard); the former could imply that many developing countries could not meet the standard for very considerable periods of time (perhaps a decade or more), while the latter may not yield much incentive for the emerging market economies to make important further improvements in their regimes.

Looking beyond international banking agreements, two-level standards are more common, especially when such agreements are meant to cover a heterogeneous group of countries. The IMF's Articles of Agreement, for example, specify that countries can adopt transitional arrangements (Article XIV status) before accepting the obligations of current-account convertibility (Article VIII status). At present, more than a third of the IMF's member countries still avail themselves of such transitional arrangements. There is an even closer parallel with the IMF's new data standards, which features a basic, transitional standard that all countries should satisfy, and a stricter standard that would apply to countries that are more heavily involved with international capital markets. Global and regional trade agreements, likewise, often specify longer transitional periods for developing countries. For example, APEC's recent "free trade" commitment calls for industrial countries to meet the target by 2010, but gives developing countries until 2020.

A similar arrangement might work for an IBS: an upper level (stricter) standard that would probably attract banks and countries more heavily involved with international capital markets and a basic (transitional) standard that would apply to all participants. The main incentive to sign on to the higher standard would be the market premium attached to having satisfied more rigorous entry qualifications. But other incentives could also be contemplated. For example, in line with supervisory arrangements in the United States, countries and banks meeting the higher standard (including higher capital requirements and stricter disclosure) could be subject to lighter supervisory oversight.

So long as subscription to an IBS is voluntary and qualification for both levels is based on objective criteria rather than merely an industrial-country/developing-country classification, administering a two-level standard might not be much harder than administering a unitary one. Also, claims of "unequal treatment" would carry less weight. If countries rather than the monitoring agency choose the level they subscribe to, the monitoring agency need not decide when to "graduate" countries from the lower level to the upper one; instead, it would reject or accept a country's application based on objective criteria for a given level.

As regards equal treatment, there is a strong case against assigning industrial countries ex ante to the upper level and developing countries to the lower one—even though the primary focus of an IBS is on improving banking systems and banking supervision in developing countries and ex post most industrial countries would probably be in the upper level and most developing ones in the lower level (at least to start). Just because the incidence of serious banking crises in industrial countries has been lower than in developing countries over the past 15 years does not mean that banking systems/banking supervision in industrial countries are free from serious shortcomings. For example, "evergreening" of bad loans (i.e., poor asset classification) and regulatory forbearance have been prominent features of the ongoing banking crisis in Japan. Heavy and misguided government involvement has been evident in the sizable public bailout of Credit Lyonnais in France. Poor preparation for financial liberalization was instrumental in the late 1980s/early 1990s banking crises in Finland, Norway, and Sweden. Poor internal controls were a key factor in the recent troubles at Daiwa and Barings. And the bitter fruits of an incentive-incompatible official safety net were dramatically illustrated in the US saving and loan crisis.[7] In short, industrial countries

---

7. See Goldstein et al. (1993) for a discussion of these industrial-country banking problems. Calomiris and White (1994) have calculated that the deposit insurance cost to taxpayers of the US saving and loan debacle exceeded in real magnitude the losses of all failed banks during the Great Depression.

should not get a free ride; they need to satisfy the same objective entry criteria as developing countries do. An IBS can therefore be a vehicle for motivating further improvements in industrial-country banking systems. Any IBS that discriminated against developing countries would not provide those countries with the proper incentives for reform. For example, if one could make the case on objective grounds that say, Hong Kong and Chile were better placed to qualify for an upper-level IBS than a few industrial countries, that differentiation should not be thwarted by some country-group classification. Following the same line of argument, it would be totally inappropriate to design an IBS only for developing countries. There can be different levels of certification, but qualification for those levels must be nondiscriminatory.

While I believe that a two-level IBS would be superior to a unitary standard, the latter would be much better than having no IBS at all.

What Should an IBS Include?

To be truly comprehensive, an IBS would need to specify guidelines for all the important aspects of banking supervision, including, inter alia: deposit insurance; lender-of-last resort operations; bank licensing and permissible banking activities; external audits; internal controls and internal audits; information requirements of bank supervisors; public disclosure; limits on large exposures and connected lending; capital adequacy; asset valuation and provisioning; foreign-exchange exposures; on-site banking inspections; legal powers and political independence of bank supervisors; the mix between rules and discretion in the implementation of corrective actions; globally consolidated supervision; cooperation (including exchange of information) between home- and host-country supervisors; and measures to combat money laundering.[8] In addition, one would want to offer some guidance on the relevant infrastructure for good banking, including: interbank and government securities markets; payments, delivery, and settlement systems; and the legal and judicial framework.

Clearly, analysis of each of these elements would go beyond the scope of this study. I will therefore concentrate on *eight priority elements of an IBS, selected primarily for their past and potential contribution to banking crises in developing countries.* For each element, I attempt to convey the flavor of what should be required, along with some indication of which provisions might be reserved for the stricter (upper-level) standard (if an IBS were designed as a two-level standard rather than a unitary one).

---

8. For an excellent analysis of "best practice" in each of these supervisory dimensions, see IMF (1997a).

Public Disclosure

IBS participants should be required to publish timely and accurate information on the financial condition of banks so that both sophisticated professional investors and less sophisticated retail depositors can make an informed assessment of bank performance and profitability. At a minimum, such information should include a balance sheet, income statement, large off-balance-sheet exposures, and summary of major concentrations of credit and market risk.[9]

This material should be prepared on a globally consolidated basis, in accordance with international accounting standards, and should be audited by a reliable independent external auditor.[10] There should be enough detail so that readers can gauge the breakdown between interest and noninterest income and expenses, the relationship between nonperforming loans and loan-loss provisions, how well or poorly the bank is capitalized, and how profitable the bank is relative to its competitors (as revealed by traditional indicators, such as the return on equity, the return on assets, etc.). If a common format for such public disclosure of banks could be agreed, this, like a common international accounting standard, would be most welcome (since it would both reduce transaction costs and facilitate comparisons among banks within and across countries). IBS participants would agree to review their legal codes to ensure that banks are liable for serious penalties if they are found to have been issuing false or misleading information to the public.

For upper-level status, banks could also be required to display prominently their most recent ratings from internationally recognized credit-rating agencies (including any downgradings). If they have not been rated, banks should disclose that fact. Upper-level participants would also commit to adopting public disclosure recommendations (jointly agreed by the Basle Committee, IOSCO, and the Eurocurrency Standing Committee) on the trading and derivative activities of banks and securities firms.[11]

Appendix D provides two examples of good public disclosure—one for the banking system as a whole and one for individual banks. The first

---

9. Later in this chapter, I introduce two additional disclosure requirements for IBS participation, specifically related to the problems of government involvement in the banking system and connected lending.

10. One problem here is that there are presently two competing international accounting standards: International Accounting Standards as drawn up by the International Accounting Standards Committee and Generally Accepted Accounting Principles (GAAP) used in the United States. See W. White (1996) for a discussion of their relative advantages and disadvantages. Discussions are ongoing among accounting bodies in the major industrial countries to see if agreement can be reached on a single international accounting standard. In the interim, use of either GAAP or international accounting standards might be acceptable for an IBS.

11. See Basle Committee on Banking Supervision (1996) for an explanation of this disclosure agreement.

shows the aggregate data published quarterly for 3,000 national banks in the United States, while the second gives the disclosure requirements for individual banks under New Zealand's new supervisory regime.[12]

Accounting and Legal Framework

The aim here should be to move closer to internationally recognized loan classification and provisioning practices and remove undesirable legal impediments to the pledging, transfer, and seizure of loan collateral and to the statutory authority of supervisors to carry out their mandate.

IBS participants would agree to set out clearly the criteria and rules/practices they employ to classify loans, provision for loan losses, and suspend accrual for overdue interest. In classifying loans, participants would agree to give appropriate weight to an assessment of the borrower's current repayment capacity, to the market value of collateral, and to the borrower's past record, and they would not rely exclusively on the loan's payment status.[13] Participants would also pledge to discourage and monitor accounting devices that facilitate the "evergreening" of bad loans.[14] The time a loan could be in arrears before it was classified as nonperforming would be no longer than 150 days. For upper-level status, that time period could be 90 days. Each participant should have mandatory provisioning rules against bad loans. For upper-level status, participants would agree to meet an international provisioning standard (if one can be agreed); pending such an agreement, upper-level participants would maintain a provisioning coverage ratio (of loan-loss reserves to nonperforming loans) not more than 10 percent below the Organization for Economic Cooperation and Development (OECD) average for the previous five-year period.

On the legal side, IBS participants would review their legal and commercial codes to certify that laws governing bankruptcy and recovery and pledging of collateral (for bank loans) do not impose undue costs on

---

12. Note that disclosure requirements for banks in New Zealand are more demanding than those in most other industrial countries, and that New Zealand's new supervisory regime places greater reliance on public disclosure (relative to prudential requirements) to discipline banks than do regimes in other industrial countries. It is sometimes argued that New Zealand can afford to rely so much on disclosure because large banks in New Zealand are foreign owned and thus subject to supervision in their home country.

13. See Meltzer (1995) for a description and analysis of how Chile strengthened its asset classification and provisioning regime.

14. De Juan (1996, 101) highlights three signs of "evergreening" and weak repayment capacity: ". . . (i) the financial statements of the borrower show negative net worth and/or negative cash flow; (ii) the loan has a history of consecutive rollovers, and the volume of each new loan is equal to or above the principal plus interest of the previous loan; and (iii) the principal or interest of previous loans is not paid in cash, but through refinancing facilities extended by the same creditor bank."

banks. In addition, participants would confirm the legal authority of bank supervisors to carry out their responsibilities (e.g., issuance and revocation of banking licenses, requests for information, setting of prudential guidelines/regulations, conducting on-site inspections, closure of insolvent banks, etc.).[15]

Internal Controls

Because of increased bank involvement in trading activities and the tremendous growth of complex financial instruments over the past decade, it is more difficult for bank supervisors and creditors to monitor accurately the risk profile of banks.[16] During the same period, there have been several notable failures at financial firms (e.g., Barings, Daiwa, Sumitomo) where time-honored principles of prudent risk management (e.g., separation of authority as between front- and back-office operations and awareness by senior management of the size of exposures) were violated (IMF 1996a). These developments underscore the importance of good internal controls at banks as the first line of defense against excessive risk taking—be it market risk, credit risk, legal risk, or operational risk.

Participating banks would agree to have available for inspection a clear written account of what procedures and safeguards are in place as part of their internal risk management. It should address how risks are measured and tracked in real time, which members of senior management and the board are responsible for oversight and for "pulling the plug" if actual exposures exceed prespecified limits, how exposure limits in the loan book and trading book are set, how different functional risks within the firm are segregated, how the consistency and accuracy of internal record keeping is cross-checked, the amount of capital that is available to cover losses in various risk categories, what backup there is in case of computer breakdowns or other information technology problems, and what safeguards have been introduced to discourage and detect fraud and money laundering. In addition, IBS participants should certify that a reliable, independent internal audit function is in operation. For upper-level status, participants would certify that banks with significant involvement in derivative markets are implementing the G-30 (1993) guidelines on risk management of derivatives, as well as the recommendations for

---

15. A particularly important area here is the ability of supervisors to get the data they need to evaluate a bank, including data on off-balance-sheet and off-shore activities; see IMF (1997a).

16. See BIS (1996) and IMF (1996a) for figures on the growth of the over-the-counter and exchange-traded derivative markets during the 1990s. Goldstein (1995b) and Hoenig (1996) discuss the difficulties that financial regulators face in trying not to "fall behind the curve" in an innovative global capital market. Garber (1996) provides an account of how Mexican banks in 1994 used off-shore structured notes to evade national prudential regulations on net open currency positions.

combating money laundering promulgated by the Financial Action Task Force on Money Laundering (1990).

Government Involvement

As highlighted in chapter 2, state-owned banks and burdensome developing-country government involvement in privately owned banks have drained public finances and generated inefficient resource allocation in banking services. Despite this dismal track record, it is neither realistic nor desirable that an IBS call for immediate privatization of all state-owned banks or mandate an end to all policy-directed lending in developing countries. After all, almost all countries have at some time intervened to influence the allocation of bank credit for what they deemed socially desirable purposes. Also, there may well be situations in developing countries where some government involvement can be legitimately defended.

But what an IBS can do is bring greater transparency and accountability to government ownership and involvement in the banking system. This should subject such operations to greater public scrutiny and make it more difficult to use the banking system as a quasi-fiscal device to circumvent legislative and political constraints on the budget. Moreover, an IBS can encourage financial institutions that operate with policy-based lending constraints to give greater weight to commercial considerations in their credit decisions, to avoid costly future bailouts. And an IBS can even ask governments to consider more carefully whether privatization of some or most of their state-owned banks would not be in their long-term interest.

Toward this end, IBS participants would agree to

- include in the government budget all government costs and quasi-fiscal operations that involve the banking system (as recently recommended by the IMF [1996b]);[17]

- annually publish data on nonperforming loans in state-owned banks (on a basis that permits comparison with privately owned banks);

- disclose the nature and extent of government instructions to banks on the allocation of credit (be it in state-owned or privately owned banks);

- subject state-owned banks to an external audit by a private independent external auditor and publish the results of that audit; and

- direct state-owned banks to give due attention to creditworthiness in their lending decisions.[18]

---

17. Mackenzie and Stella (1996) explain how one might define and measure quasi-fiscal operations of public financial institutions.

18. Kaufman (1996a) urges developing countries where state-owned banks account for an important share of total bank assets to recapitalize all banks so that they are market-value

For upper-level status, countries where state-owned banks account for a significant share of total banking assets would agree to review the costs and benefits of their state-owned banks, with an eye toward assessing the scope for privatization of such institutions.

Connected Lending

IBS participants would establish an exposure limit on lending to connected parties, endorse the principle that lending to connected parties should be on terms that are no more favorable than those extended to nonrelated borrowers of a similar risk class, outlaw practices that make it difficult or impossible for supervisors to verify the accuracy of reported connected-lending exposure (e.g., use of fictitious names, dummy corporations, etc.), and publicly disclose the share of loans going to connected parties and the identity of large shareholders and their affiliations.[19] For upper-level status, participants would establish below-maximum-limit threshold reporting limits (to bank supervisors) on connected lending (to give supervisors advance warning of rapidly rising exposure to connected lending).

Bank Capital

Signatories to an IBS would adopt the existing 8 percent risk-weighted capital standard for credit risk, along with the recent amendment for market risk. To reflect the need for higher capital when the operating environment is relatively volatile, countries seeking upper-level status would apply a "safety factor" if their recent history of loan defaults, restructured loans, and/or government assistance to troubled banks was significantly higher than the OECD average over say, the past five years. This safety factor could possibly involve multiplying the level I capital requirement by 1.5, so that "volatile" countries would apply a minimum risk-weighted capital standard for credit risk of 12 percent. This approach would respect the principle of equal treatment. Any country—industrial or developing—that had a relatively volatile operating environment for its banks would apply the higher requirement if it wanted to meet the upper-level standard. Also, a country's actions to reduce that volatility

---

solvent, privatize to improve the incentives for banks and to reduce political pressures, put in place an incentive-compatible safety net, and resist or minimize nonprudential regulations that focus on political, social, or other objectives.

19. Exposure limits on connected lending should be additional to those on maximum exposure to a single borrower. According to a recent survey of the Basle Committee (Padoa-Schioppa 1996), 90 percent of countries do not allow lending to a single customer to exceed 60 percent of the bank's capital, and roughly two-thirds of countries maintain the stricter exposure limit of 25 percent of capital. See Goldstein and Turner (1996) for the exposure limits on single borrowers in a group of emerging economies.

(e.g., more stable macroeconomic policies) would, if sustained, eventually be reflected by a lower capital requirement. Much of this parallels the Basle Committee's approach to determination of regulatory capital for market risk (Basle Committee on Banking Supervision 1996; Padoa-Schioppa 1996).

An Incentive Compatible Safety Net and Resisting Pressures for Regulatory Forbearance

The aim here should be to retain the positive features of an official safety net for banks (i.e., discouragement of bank runs and limitation of systemic risk) while reducing its negative (moral hazard) effects (i.e., less market discipline from bank creditors, excessive risk taking by banks, increased costs for taxpayers, and delay in enforcing corrective actions on undercapitalized banks by financial regulators). To do that, the safety net must incorporate incentives that tilt the behavior of the main players in the right direction.

The most promising approach to date for designing an incentive-compatible official safety net is the system of structured early intervention and resolution (SEIR), put forward by Benston and Kaufman (1988) in the late 1980s and incorporated with some modifications in US banking legislation in the early 1990s.[20] The losses (at least $150 billion) incurred in the saving and loan debacle and the prospect of similar difficulties for US commercial banks supplied the political motivation for reform. The key legislative vehicle was the Federal Deposit Insurance Corporation Improvement Act (FDICIA) of 1991. The underlying strategy has two pillars: first, to maintain deposit insurance for banks but to use regulatory sanctions to mimic the penalties that the private market would impose on banks (as their financial condition deteriorated) if they were not insured, and second, to reduce greatly the discretion that regulators have in imposing both corrective actions and closure of a bank.

The safety-net reforms embodied in FDICIA legislation can be summarized as follows: (1) government deposit insurance is retained for small depositors;[21] (2) deposit insurance premiums paid by banks are risk weight-

---

20. Benston and Kaufman (1996) argue that while FDICIA was a big step forward in deposit-insurance reform, it should have set the capital-zone thresholds higher, used a simple leverage ratio to measure capital (rather than using both this ratio and the Basle risk-weighted one), embraced market-value accounting, established stiffer penalties for Federal Reserve lending through the discount window to banks that subsequently failed, made wider spreads between the deposit insurance premiums paid by the safest and riskiest banks, and given even less scope for discretion in applying prompt corrective action and least cost resolution.

21. The rationale for covering small depositors is that they might otherwise run into currency when banks get into trouble, they are generally less adept than large bank creditors in evaluating the true financial condition of banks, and they have enough political muscle

ed (depending on their capital and bank examination rating); (3) banks become subject to progressively harsher regulatory sanctions (e.g., eliminating dividends, restricting asset growth, and changing management) as their capital falls below multiple capital-zone tripwires; (4) by the same token, well capitalized banks receive "carrots" in the form of wider bank powers and lighter regulatory oversight; (5) regulators' discretion is sharply curtailed (with respect to initiating "prompt corrective actions" and resolving a critically undercapitalized bank at least cost to the insurance fund (least cost resolution); (6) effective 1 January 1995 the insurance fund is generally prohibited from protecting uninsured depositors or creditors at a failed bank if this would increase the loss to the deposit insurance fund; and (7) provision is made for a discretionary, systemic-risk override to protect all depositors in exceptional circumstances (when not doing so "would have serious adverse effects on economic conditions or financial stability")—but activation of this override requires explicit, unanimous approval by the most senior economic officials and subjects any bailout to increased accountability (Benston and Kaufman 1988, 1996; Kaufman 1996a, 1996b). Table 3.1 summarizes the prompt-corrective-action features of FDICIA.

Proponents of SEIR argue that it improves incentives on at least five counts (Benston and Kaufman 1996; Kaufman 1996b). Because uninsured creditors of banks realize they will be at the end of the queue if a bank gets into trouble, they will monitor banks more assiduously, thereby enhancing market discipline. Because bank owners and managers know the penalties in advance if losses are sustained and banks become undercapitalized, they will be less inclined to engage in excessive risk taking and will not allow bank capital to fall too low. Because bank supervisors are largely obliged to prompt corrective action and least cost resolution, they will be less susceptible to pressures for regulatory forbearance. Because the most senior economic officials know that granting "too large to fail" assistance requires unanimous approval and involves increased public scrutiny, they will be dissuaded from doing so unless there is a clear systemic threat at hand. And because the explicit closure rule calls for resolving a failed bank while it still has positive net worth, losses to the deposit insurance fund should be small (thereby making it less costly to keep the fund fully funded).[22] In contrast, safety-net regimes that do not incorporate SEIR often leave a key question unanswered: What happens when bank capital drops below the regulatory standard?

---

anyway to force the government to bailout their losses if they were not covered by insurance (Kaufman 1996a).

22. If the deposit insurance scheme lacks sufficient financial resources, even insured depositors may be tempted to run during periods of bank weakness; moreover, regulators will be more inclined to grant regulatory forbearance because there are insufficient resources to liquidate the bank.

Table 3.1 Summary of prompt-corrective-action provisions of the federal Deposit Insurance Corporation Improvement Act of 1991

Zone	Mandatory provisions	Discretionary provisions	Risk-based total	Risk-based tier 1	Leverage tier 1
1. Well capitalized			>10	>6	>5
2. Adequately capitalized	1. No brokered deposits, except with FDIC approval		>8	>4	>4
3. Undercapitalized	1. Suspend dividends and management fees 2. Require capital restoration plan 3. Restrict asset growth 4. Approval required for acquisitions, branching, and new activities 5. No brokered deposits	1. Order recapitalization 2. Restrict interaffiliate transactions 3. Restrict deposit interest rates 4. Restrict certain other activities 5. Any other action that would better carry out prompt corrective action	<8	<4	<4
4. Significantly undercapitalized	1. Same as for zone 3 2. Order recapitalization[a] 3. Restrict interaffiliate transactions[a] 4. Restrict deposit interest rates[a] 5. Pay of officers restricted	1. Any zone 3 discretionary actions 2. Conservatorship or receivership if it fails to submit or implement a plan or recapitalize pursuant to order 3. Any other zone 5 provision, if such action is necessary to carry out prompt corrective action	<6	<3	<3

48

5. Critically undercapitalized   <2

1. Same as for zone 4
2. Receiver/conservator within 90 days[a]
3. Receiver if still in zone 5 four quarters after becoming critically undercapitalized
4. Suspend payments on subordinated debt[a]
5. Restrict certain other activities

a. Not required if primary supervisor determines action would not serve purpose of prompt corrective action, or if certain other conditions are met.

Source: Board of Governors of the Federal Reserve.

As acknowledged by Benston and Kaufman (1996), FDICIA has been in operation for only five years, the US economy has not undergone a major cyclical downturn during that period, and no US money-center bank has become critically undercapitalized during this period. In addition, broader economic factors have no doubt contributed to the recovery of the US banks and S&Ls. It is, therefore, too early to come to a definitive verdict on the effectiveness of FDICIA. Nevertheless, the preliminary signs are encouraging. Not only are bank failures and bank problems down and bank capital and profitability up, but as shown in table 3.2, a much higher share of uninsured depositors has gone unprotected since FDICIA came on stream. This is a strong signal that market discipline is beginning to bite.

Some exporting of FDICIA is already going on. In drawing lessons from its recent/ongoing banking difficulties, Japan plans to establish a prompt-corrective-action system in April 1998, and the banking laws of some developing countries (e.g., Chile) contain significant precommitment features. With no superior alternatives out there for reforming official safety nets, FDICIA-like features (to combat moral hazard and regulatory forbearance) ought also be included in an IBS. For example, IBS participants could agree to make some corrective actions mandatory if bank capital dropped below the regulatory minimum, ensure there is a well defined closure rule/procedure for banks, make it publicly known that uninsured creditors (including sellers of interbank funds) stand behind insured depositors and the deposit insurance fund in being protected from bank losses, and require that granting of "too large to fail" emergency financial assistance to banks be publicly approved by both the governor of the central bank and the minister of finance.

Consolidated Supervision and Cooperation Among Host- and Home-Country Supervisors

The Basle Committee on Banking Supervision has been on target in insisting that (1) all international banks be supervised on a globally consolidated basis by a capable home-country supervisor; (2) home-country supervisors be able to gather information from their cross-border banking establishments; (3) before a cross-border banking establishment is created, it receive prior consent from both the host- and home-country authorities; and (4) host countries have recourse to certain defensive actions (e.g., prohibit the establishment of banking offices) if they determine that conditions (1)-(3) are not being satisfied (Basle Committee on Banking Supervision 1996). Participants in an IBS should therefore agree to implement the 1992 Basle Minimum Standards.

Could an IBS be Agreed on?

So much for the makeup of an IBS. But wouldn't an IBS represent such an ambitious extension of existing international banking agreements as

Table 3.2 FDIC banks' resolutions, 1986–95 (by protection of loss of uninsured depositors)

Year	Number of banks				Total assets (billions of dollars)			
	Total	Protected	Not protected	Percentage not protected	Total	Protected	Not protected	Percentage not protected
1986	145	102	40	28	7.6	6.3	1.3	17
1987	203	152	51	25	9.2	6.7	2.5	27
1988	221	185	36	16	52.6	51.3	1.3	3
1989	207	176	31	15	29.4	27.2	2.2	8
1990	169	149	20	12	15.8	13.3	2.5	16
1991	127	106	21	17	62.5	60.9	1.6	3
1992	122	56	66	54	45.5	25.0	20.5	45
1993	41	6	35	85	3.5	0.2	3.3	94
1994	13	5	8	62	1.4	0.6	0.8	57
1995	6	0	6	100	0.8	0.0	0.8	100

Source: Benston and Kaufman (1996).

to preclude agreement? After all, several of these items were no doubt raised in the Basle Committee in previous years without garnering the requisite support. If agreement could not be reached among the G-10 countries, wouldn't it be unrealistic to expect agreement on a wider list of banking reforms among a broader group of countries?

I find this criticism unpersuasive. Prior to the Mexican economic crisis of late 1994 to 1995, few would have anticipated reaching agreement on an international standard for publication of economic and financial data (the IMF's SDDS), or on doubling the IMF's line of credit from the General Agreement to Borrow and its extension to 14 new member countries, or on establishing a concerted official position on the rescheduling of sovereign bank debt (the so-called "orderly workout" issue). Yet, barely two years after the onset of the Mexican crisis, the international community has reached agreement on all three (Goldstein 1996b).

In analyzing past international agreements in the area of financial stability, Kapstein (1992) identifies three underlying factors: a shared recognition of a common problem, some agreement on how the financial system should function and how problems might best be addressed, and the continuing exercise of state power to make it happen. It is only within the last year or two, with the publication of several comprehensive studies, that the scope and severity of banking problems in developing countries has come to be more widely appreciated, particularly by observers in the G-10 countries (Lindgren, Garcia, and Saal 1996; Caprio and Klingebiel 1996a, 1996b; Honohan 1996). And, it is only recently that research has produced a reasonable consensus on the factors behind these banking crises and the policy changes that would help to alleviate the problem (Caprio and Klingebiel 1996a, 1996b; Goldstein 1996a; Goldstein and Turner 1996; Kane 1995; Kaufman 1996a; Meltzer 1995; Rojas-Suarez and Weisbrod 1995, 1996a, 1996b, 1996c, 1996d). As regards leadership from the official sector, it was only at the Lyon Summit in June 1996 that G-7 heads of state (G-7 1996, 3) put the "... adoption of strong prudential standards in emerging economies" on their crisis prevention agenda, and it has been primarily during the past six months that senior international policymakers have begun to stress the need for a coordinated international approach to banking problems in developing countries (G-7 1996; Camdessus 1996; Summers 1996; Pou 1996). In short, each of Kapstein's (1992) criteria for agreement are considerably closer to being satisfied now than they were even three years ago. What could be agreed then is not necessarily what can be agreed now.

Who Should Set the IBS?

Since more robust banking systems and more effective banking supervision would be in their common interest, an IBS ought to be sponsored jointly by the international financial institutions (the IMF, World Bank, and BIS), the Basle Committee on Banking Supervision, regulatory and supervisory authorities from the developing world, and representatives of the banking industry. But who should set the specific guidelines for an IBS?

The main expertise needed to draft an IBS is banking supervision. This suggests that the Basle Committee on Banking Supervision should play a key role in the exercise, that is, they should draft the key provisions of the IBS that relate specifically to banking supervision. The Basle Committee's leadership would give the IBS a brand name and provide a sense of continuity with earlier international banking agreements.

But the Basle Committee should not be the only group working on an IBS, for at least four reasons.

First, as outlined above, a good IBS would be somewhat broader in design (e.g., international accounting standards, greater transparency for government involvement in the banking system, etc.) than the confines of traditional banking supervision; as such, other groups that have more direct responsibility for these adjacent issues (e.g., the IASC or IMF) should be involved and their contributions folded into the final product. Such interagency collaboration would be even more essential if the ultimate aim were not merely to produce an IBS but rather to a produce a minimum international standard for, say, banking and securities activities; in that case, the guidelines of securities regulators (i.e., IOSCO) should be folded into the IBS into the broader standard. In either case, some international umbrella group at a higher level than the Basle Committee (e.g., the Interim Committee of the IMF or a working group of ministers of finance and central bank governors from larger industrial and developing countries) would need to coordinate the assembly of the final product.

Second, and pointing in the same direction, because an IBS introduces some issues not raised by earlier international banking agreements (e.g., international monitoring of national supervisory regimes), enlarges the intersection between the microeconomic and macroeconomic aspects of financial regulation, and would require large changes in banking practices in some countries, the Basle Committee's collaboration with other interested parties should be more extensive and intensive than normal. For example, if the international financial agencies (the IMF, World Bank, and regional development banks) were assigned the tasks of advising countries on how to alter their banking and supervisory arrangements to conform to an IBS, of monitoring participating countries' compliance with the standard (as discussed later in this chapter), and of intensifying their normal financial surveillance and financial-sector restructuring work, then their views ought to be sought as to whether any guidelines drawn up by the Basle Committee are sufficiently specific and comprehensive. Their views would be particularly valuable on whether any consensus on an IBS reached in the Basle Committee had ducked some of the tough issues (e.g., whether countries with volatile operating environments should have higher regulatory capital requirements, whether an IBS includes incentives that will reduce over time government involvement in the banking system, etc.) that are apt to be crucial in reducing the vulnerability of developing-country banking systems. Given BIS's considerable expertise in the intersection of the micro and macroeconomic elements of financial regulation, it should likewise be accorded an important role in reviewing any draft IBS guidelines produced by the Basle Committee.

Third, the banking industry needs to be given ample opportunity to record its views on what elements should and should not be included in an IBS; after all, it is the banking industry that would need to absorb any costs associated with meeting the requirements of an IBS. The influence of their input should not be minimized. For example, the decision by the Basle Committee to permit banks to employ their own internal risk-management models to help calculate regulatory capital requirements for market risk occurred only after banks in several larger industrial countries expressed their dissatisfaction with the earlier proposal to base these capital requirements on a preset formula.[23]

Fourth, the group that sets the IBS should have strong representation from developing countries. Since developing-country banking systems and banking supervision are the primary focus of the IBS exercise, the drafting group needs to have firsthand experience with developing-country banking supervision issues. Without that experience, the IBS guidelines are not likely to be as well suited to the practical banking problems faced by developing countries as they could be with strong representation from these countries. Without adequate support from the developing countries, an IBS is unlikely to get off the ground. Some groups in developing countries are likely to resist the banking reforms necessary to qualify for IBS admission; some may even argue that an IBS is a scheme by industrial countries and their banks to reduce the competitiveness of developing-country banks by imposing onerous prudential standards—standards that many industrial countries will already have met or exceeded. Spokespersons for banking reform in developing countries will be better able to overcome opposition and convince their publics and their banking industries that such (voluntary) reforms are in the best interest of their country if they can legitimately say that they were full participants in drafting an IBS. Although the Basle Committee presently includes only bank supervisors from G-10 countries, there is no reason why the working group that drafts the IBS should not include significant representation from developing countries. Developing-country representatives should also serve on any other working groups that are contributing to an IBS.

---

23. See IMF (1995) for a discussion of this background to the recent amendment of the Basle Capital Adequacy Accord to cover market risk.

In the end, after the interagency collaboration is complete, there must be full agreement on the guidelines in an IBS. If, for example, the IMF and World Bank had a different view on minimum standards for accounting and provisioning than did the Basle Committee, countries participating in an IBS would not understand their obligations and the monitoring process would be unnecessarily complicated. When the smoke clears, there can be only one IBS.[24]

How Should Compliance with an IBS Be Monitored and Encouraged?

This is probably the single toughest operational issue facing an IBS. There are basically two approaches.

The traditional one, at least in the field of international banking agreements, is to have international recommendations ratified by ministers and governors, incorporated into national law or regulation, and then monitored/enforced by the national banking supervisor (W. White 1996). This approach has its advantages. By maintaining home-country control, the chances that reforms are "owned" by the home country are maximized, and the criticism that conditions are being imposed by an international agency are avoided. Also, national supervisors are apt to be more knowledgeable about local banking conditions than an outside group would be.

The rub is that exclusive home-country control will weaken the implementation/credibility of an IBS in those countries where weak banking supervision is part of the problem. In those cases, an independent outside monitor should render an objective evaluation of whether an IBS is being implemented as agreed. A hint of the complacency that might be associated with home-country monitoring is offered by a recent Basle Committee survey (Padoa-Schioppa 1996), which covered 129 countries: two-thirds of the countries reported that the supervisory agency is independent from the government; only 13 countries acknowledged that their banks grant loans in compliance with governmental directives; 72 percent of nonindustrial countries responded that they do not allow lending to a single customer to exceed 25 percent of the bank's capital; and over 90 percent of all countries reported that supervisors verify the adequacy of bank's accounting systems. It makes you wonder. Either all those studies showing political pressures on supervisors, government-directed lending, connected lending, and weak accounting systems to be major factors in banking crises were wrong (BIS 1996; Caprio and Klingebiel 1996a, 1996b;

---

24. This is not to say that in their financial surveillance and financial restructuring work, the IMF and the World Bank should not address areas that are not covered in an IBS. But for the areas that are covered, everyone has to be singing from the same hymn book.

Folkerts-Landau et al. 1995; Goldstein and Turner 1996; Honohan 1996; Lindgren, Garcia, and Saal 1996; Meltzer 1995; Rojas-Suarez and Weisbrod 1996a, 1996b, 1996c, 1996d; Sheng 1996), or there has recently been a tremendous improvement in supervision.

The second approach is to entrust at least part of the monitoring to an international agency. This has been a long-standing practice in the areas of trade policy, macroeconomic stabilization, and sectoral reform (including the financial sector); note the roles of the General Agreement on Tariffs and Trade (GATT)-World Trade Organization (WTO), IMF, World Bank, and regional development banks (e.g., European Bank for Reconstruction and Development, Inter-American Development Bank, Asian Development Bank, etc.). Here, countries have decided that, despite the dilution of home-country control, evaluation by an international agency is critical to the agreement's credibility.

But which international agency or agencies should do the monitoring? I believe the IMF and the World Bank group are the most logical candidates. Only they have the universal membership that would include all potential participants in an IBS. Also, monitoring compliance with an IBS would require on-site inspections and discussions with local supervisory authorities and local banks. The IMF and the World Bank already send missions to countries and only they currently have enough personnel to make on-site visits throughout the developing world. I envision the Bretton Woods institutions carrying out at least three functions associated with an IBS.

First, the World Bank and regional development banks could incorporate the IBS guidelines into the training, technical assistance, and financial restructuring advice that they already provide to many countries. In this sense, the IBS would help guide banking system reform in developing countries and delineate the banking-system preconditions that are necessary for developing countries to benefit from greater financial integration.[25]

Second, the IMF could carry the primary responsibility for determining whether countries voluntarily subscribing to the IBS were meeting their obligations. They would base that determination on off-site analysis and information obtained during missions (on-site) to the country. During those missions, they would hold discussions with national bank supervisors and a sample of local banks. National banking supervisors would continue to have the primary oversight responsibility for their banks but the mission would seek to reach a view, inter alia, as to whether national banking supervision itself was implementing faithfully the IBS guidelines. If a determination was made that a country was not meeting its IBS responsibilities, it could be given a fixed period of time to remedy the

25. See the recent World Bank report (1997) for an extensive discussion of the preconditions for successful financial integration.

situation. If the country displayed serious and persistent nonobservance of the IBS guidelines, then the IMF would indicate publicly that the country's subscription to the IBS was suspended. Like the IMF's SDDS, an electronic bulletin board could be established on the internet listing those countries that subscribed to the IBS and were in good standing; persistent noncompliance would be signaled by taking a country "off the board."

This option of taking a noncomplying IBS member off the board is necessary to give the IBS credibility with private capital markets. If there are no significant penalties for not behaving as a good club member, then club membership will not yield a market return. That said, it would be a mistake for the IMF to create the impression that an IBS member of good standing is immune to banking problems. As laid out in chapter 2, banking-sector vulnerability depends on a number of factors in addition to banking supervision, including the state of the macroeconomy and the appropriateness of the country's exchange rate policy; the IBS does not address those sources of vulnerability and implying otherwise would only lead to a downgrading of the monitoring agency's credibility. Instead, the IMF should make it clear that being an IBS member in good standing carries a much narrower interpretation—namely, that the country is meeting IBS minimum standards of good banking supervision.

Third, the IMF and the World Bank could provide further incentive for signing on to the IBS and honoring its obligations by factoring compliance with the IBS guidelines into their policy conditionality decisions and/or by publishing their analysis of banking-sector developments.

By including compliance with IBS guidelines as an element of policy conditionality, the IMF in its stabilization programs and the World Bank in its financial restructuring programs would give those countries seeking financial assistance a further incentive to undertake banking reform. From the perspective of the international financial institutions (IFIs), there is good reason for such conditionality: if nothing is done to overcome banking-sector fragility, other elements of stabilization and financial reform could be rendered ineffective and the IFIs' chances of being repaid on time diminished. Also, at least in crisis situations, some banking system reforms are presumably already part of Bretton Woods conditionality; the IBS guidelines would just bring a more widely accepted framework to that element of conditionality. On the negative side, the more the IBS guidelines become a requirement, the less one captures the aforementioned advantages of a voluntary standard. Also, this additional source of leverage would only apply to countries seeking financial assistance from the IMF and the World Bank. On top of that, the potential ambiguities of judging compliance with an IBS that contains many elements should not be underestimated.

Rather than simply conveying an "on-off" signal to the private capital markets about IBS membership (i.e., country x is or is not a member in good standing of the IBS), the IMF could publish a more informative signal—its analysis of banking-sector developments and the quality of banking supervision in individual countries. The IBS guidelines could then serve as a useful organizing device for such reports. Presumably, such an analysis would be included with an analysis of monetary, fiscal, and structural policies, in the IMF's Article IV consultation report for the country. Again, such a monitoring role would affect incentives via its effect on information flows to private capital markets and ultimately on the country's cost of borrowing in those markets.

Whether it would be desirable to release to the markets that part of IMF consultation reports containing the staff's analysis of economic policies and prospects has been hotly debated for at least a decade, and publishing an assessment of banking system soundness focusing on IBS benchmarks raises a similar debate; that is, enhanced market discipline versus concerns about precipitating crises and reducing the frankness of IMF consultations. Although the choice is not an easy one, I have concluded elsewhere (Goldstein 1995a) that, on balance, there is much more to be gained than lost from publishing Article IV reports, and I would extend that conclusion to analyses of banking systems as well.

At least three criticisms might be leveled against such a monitoring role for the IFIs.

For one thing, it can be argued that IFIs do not have enough personnel with the requisite training and experience to make reliable evaluations of banking systems and banking supervision. This criticism carries some currency but should become less relevant over the medium term. Both the World Bank and the IMF have gained valuable and wide-ranging experience in assessing and providing technical assistance on developing-country banking systems. Yet, if an IBS were agreed on, their increased responsibilities in this area would no doubt require additional staff with banking supervisory expertise. This will take some time. In the interim, some assistance might come from short-term loans of bank supervisors from G-10 countries and from those emerging-market economies with more advanced supervisory systems.

A second line of criticism is that the IFIs are too politicized to make the hard decision of taking a nonperforming IBS member country off the board. But the IFIs have shown a willingness over several decades to interrupt their loans to countries under stabilization and restructuring programs when the latter have failed to meet agreed on performance criteria (a decision that can also generate significant effects in private capital markets). Why should suspension from the IBS be different in kind?

Yet a third objection is that having the IFIs comment—perhaps even publicly—on the performance of national bank supervisors would compromise the latter's independence and effectiveness. I find this argument unconvincing. To begin with, there *is* something to criticize. As detailed in chapter 2, there is no precedent for the wave of severe banking crises that have enveloped developing countries over the past 15 years; likewise, there have been some serious breakdowns in banking supervision in industrial countries, including that surrounding the current Japanese banking problem. Moreover, the contention that banking crises had little to do with banking supervision does not seem to be supported by existing analysis. Caprio and Klingebiel (1996b), for example, studied the factors contributing to 29 severe developing-country banking crises from 1980 to 1996 and concluded that poor supervision and regulation (broadly defined) were instrumental in more crises than were any other factor (e.g., recessions, declines in the terms of trade, fraud, lending to state enterprises, political interference, and deficient bank management). Also, one should not confuse independence with immunity from IFI criticism. For example, IMF and OECD publications have long provided an assessment of national monetary and fiscal policies (including evaluation of the monetary policies of independent central banks), without any claims that such assessments reduce the effectiveness of national authorities. Why then should national banking supervision receive a "special" exemption from such international surveillance?[26] Indeed, with serious banking problems continuing to surface at disarming frequency (note the recent problems in South Korea and Thailand) and with weak national banking supervision identified as an important contributory factor, it seems incumbent to ask, "Who's supervising the supervisors?"

---

26. Another possible instrument for international assessment of national supervisory policies would be "peer review" within the Basle Committee. While this would probably be some improvement over what we have now, such an exercise could easily succumb to "nonaggression pacts" that essentially eliminate criticism. See Bergsten and Henning (1996) on how such nonaggression pacts have reduced the effectiveness of peer pressure within the G-7.

4

Concluding Remarks and an Action Agenda

Gone are the days when efforts to prevent international financial crises could focus almost exclusively on the industrial countries. In the wake of the Mexican economic crisis, the official sector has moved decisively to fortify the existing crisis prevention/management architecture by obtaining agreement on a new international standard for the publication of economic and financial data, doubling the size of the IMF's emergency credit line from creditor countries (the New Arrangements to Borrow and the General Agreement to Borrow), and clarifying the "rules of the game" for the resolution of sovereign liquidity crises.

But the largest gap in existing crisis prevention arrangements has yet to be filled. The last 15 years have witnessed an unprecedented wave of banking crises in developing countries. Current international banking agreements were not designed to deal with most of the major sources of banking crises in developing countries. Nor is it likely that technical assistance and/or market discipline will on their own be capable of motivating serious banking reform. A voluntary international banking standard offers a way to increase the scope and pace of banking reform in both developing and industrial countries. An IBS will not end banking crises—that is not a realistic objective. But if an IBS lowered the frequency of serious banking crises, the potential payoff would be significant.

During the past nine months, the scope and severity of the banking problem in developing countries seem to have become visible on the radar screens of policymakers. At the Lyon Economic Summit in June 1996, G-7 heads of state asked their officials to make maximum progress on ". . . encouraging the adoption of strong prudential standards in emerging economies," and to report on this progress at the June 1997 G-7 Economic Summit in Denver. In keeping with that mandate, over the next few months the Basle Committee on Banking Supervision, the IMF, and a joint G-10/developing-country working group most likely will each issue reports on banking supervision and financial stability in emerging-market economies. It is likely that each of these three reports will contain a list of minimum or best-practice guidelines on banking supervision. What then should be the next steps?

In the next six months leading up to the Denver G-7 Summit and 1997 IMF-World Bank Annual Meeting in Hong Kong, four tasks should be high on the policy agenda.

First, the sets of banking guidelines coming out of the Basle Committee, IMF, and joint G-10/developing-country working group need to be analyzed and debated, with the aim of reaching a consensus within the official sector on which individual guidelines should be accorded the highest priority and merged into a consensus IBS. As part of that debate and search for common ground, the guidelines put forward by the official sector ought to be compared to those produced by independent outside experts, such as the IBS proposal advanced in this study. Such a comparison would determine whether the guidelines suggested by the official sector have tackled the most thorny problems that have been so prevalent in past developing-country banking crises, specifically: Do those guidelines encourage the kind of public disclosure that would enhance market discipline? Do they call for an end to lax asset classification and provisioning practices? Do they suggest mechanisms that over time will reduce excessive government involvement in the banking system? Do they call for higher capital for banks operating in countries with volatile environments? Do they reform incentives in official safety nets? Do they establish countervailing protection against pressures for regulatory forbearance? And do they provide for international monitoring of those guidelines, along with a mechanism to disqualify countries that are not meeting their obligations? If a number of these tough issues have been ducked, the official guidelines ought to be revised to include them.

Second, the commercial banking industry ought to be brought into the picture to get the benefit of its suggestions and criticisms on the design of an IBS. Are the guidelines too demanding or not demanding enough? What would be the costs to banks of implementing these reforms? Do the guidelines afford banks enough flexibility in meeting the objectives of an IBS? What are reasonable transition periods for meeting the guidelines? Should the guidelines be more like minimum standards or best practice? Which of the activities assigned to bank supervisors in an IBS could be handled better by the private market? If necessary, the draft guidelines should again be revised to take account of the banking industry's input.

Third, IFIs should intensify their discussions and preparations for implementing an IBS. If an IBS were agreed on, how could the IMF and

World Bank make best use of their competitive advantages in allocating responsibilities for implementing it? What staffing requirements would the IFIs face in advising countries on and in monitoring their compliance with an IBS? How could collaboration with the Basle Committee and national bank supervisors be strengthened? Are there ways in which the BIS and the Eurocurrency Standing Committee could contribute to a concerted effort for earlier detection of banking problems? If the IMF were to share its assessments of banking-sector problems with the private capital markets, how could that best be accomplished (without casting the IFIs into the role of bank credit-rating agencies)?

Finally, after further discussions at the Interim and Development Committee meetings in April 1997 and at the Denver G-7 Summit in June 1997, a proposal for an IBS should be taken up at the September 1997 IMF-World Bank Annual Meeting in Hong Kong. By the Hong Kong meetings, there ought to have been enough debate and revision on the IBS to put forth a consensus proposal.

That proposal should contain an opening date for countries to start subscribing to the IBS. If by that time, securities regulators (i.e., IOSCO) and the International Accounting Standards Committee have international standards of their own to put forward, consideration could even be given to folding the three sets of standards together into a broader (voluntary) international banking and securities standard.

To be sure, an IBS is an ambitious undertaking that would push banking supervisors and the IFIs beyond where they have gone before. Nevertheless, the stakes involved in reducing the frequency and severity of banking crises in the developing world and the absence of superior policy options suggest to me that we should get on with the job—and with a sense of urgency. This is the time to look for your key where you lost it—not under the lamp post.

APPENDICES

Appendix A

Table A.1 Recent IMF survey of banking problems worldwide, 1980–96

Banking Crises

Argentina	(1980–82, 1989–90, and Jan–Sep 1995)
Benin	(1988)
Bulgaria	(1991–present)
Cameroon	(1989–93, 1995–present)
Central African Republic	(1976–92)
Chad	(1979–83)
Chile	(1981–87)
Congo	(1994–present)
Equatorial Guinea	(1983–85)
Estonia	(1992–95)
Finland	(1991–94)
Guinea	(1980–85)
Jordan	(1989–90)
Kuwait	(mid-1980s)
Latvia	(1995–present)
Lebanon	(1988–90)
Liberia	(1991–95)
Lithuania	(1995–present)
Macedonia	(1993–94)
Malaysia	(1985–88)
Mexico	(1982, 1994–present)
Niger	(1983–present)
Norway	(1987–93)
Panama	(1988–89)
Philippines	(1981–87)
São Tomé and Principe	(1980–present)
Senegal	(1983–88)
Somalia	(1990)
South Africa	(1985–present)
Spain	(1977–85)
Sweden	(1990–93)
Tanzania	(1988–present)
Thailand	(1983–87)
Turkey	(1985, 1991)
Uruguay	(1981–85)
Venezuela	(1994–present)

Significant Banking Problems

Albania	(1992–present)
Algeria	(1990–92)
Angola	(1991–present)
Armenia	(1991–present)
Australia	(1989–92)

Azerbaijan	(1995–present)
Bangladesh	(1980s–present)
Belarus	(1995–present)
Bhutan	(early 1990s–present)
Bolivia	(1986–87, 1994–present)
Botswana	(1994–95)
Brazil	(1994–present)
Brunei	(mid-1980s)
Burkina Faso	1988–94)
Burundi	(1994–present)
Cambodia	(ongoing)
Canada	(1983–85)
Cape Verde	(1993–present)
Central African Republic	(1995–present)
Chad	(1992)
China	(1980s–present)[a]
Columbia	(1982–85)
Costa Rica	(mid-1994–present)
Côte d'Ivoire	(1988–90)
Croatia	(1995)
Czech Republic	(1991–present)
Denmark	(1987–92)
Djibouti	(1991–93)
Dominican Republic	(1992–present)
Ecuador	(1995–present)
Egypt	(1991–95)
El Salvador	(1989)
Equatorial Guinea	(1995)
Eritrea	(1994)
Ethiopia	(1994–95)
Fiji	(1995–present)
France	(1991–95)
Gabon	(1995–present)
Gambia	(1985–92)
Georgia	(1991–present)
Germany	(1990–93)
Ghana	(1983–89)
Greece	(1991–95)
Guinea-Bissan	(ongoing)
Guyana	(1993–95)
Haiti	(1991–present)
Hungary	(1987–present)
Iceland	(1985–86, 1993)
India	(1991–present)
Indonesia	(1992–present)
Ireland	(1985)
Israel	(1983–89)
Italy	(1990–95)
Jamaica	(1994–present)
Japan	(1992–present)
Kazakhstan	(1991–95)
Kenya	(1993)
Korea, South	(mid-1980s)
Kuwait	(1990–91)

(continued next page)

Table A.1 (continued)

Kyrgyzstan	(ongoing)
Laos	(early 1990s)
Lesotho	(1988–present)
Madagascar	(1988, 1991–95)
Mali	(1987–89, 1995)
Mauritania	(1991–93)
Moldova	(1994–present)
Mongolia	(1991–present)
Mozambique	(1988–93, 1994–95)
Myanmar	(ongoing)
Nepal	(late 1980s–present)
New Zealand	(1988–90)
Nicaragua	(late 1980s–present)
Nigeria	(1991–95)
Pakistan	(1980–present)
Papua New Guinea	(1989–present)
Paraguay	(1995–present)
Peru	(1983–90)
Poland	(1991–present)
Romania	(1990–present)
Russia	(1992–present)
Rwanda	(1991–present)
Sierra Leone	(1990–present)
Slovak Republic	(1991–95)
Slovenia	(1992–94)
Sri Lanka	(early 1990s)
St. Vincent and the Grenadines	(1994–present)
Swaziland	(1995)
Tajikistan	(ongoing)
Togo	(1989–91)
Trinidad and Tobago	(1982–93)
Tunisia	(1991–95)
Turkey	(1994)
Uganda	(1990–present)
Ukraine	(1994–present)
United States	(1980–92)
Uzbekistan	(1993–present)
Vietnam	(ongoing)
Yemen Arab Republic	(ongoing)
Zaire	(1991–present)
Zambia	(1994–present)
Zimbabwe	(1995–present)

Note: Banking crises are cases where there were runs or other substantial portfolio shifts, massive government intervention, or collapses of financial firms. Significant banking problems refer to cases where there was extensive banking unsoundness short of a crisis.

a. In 1995, fraud resulted in major losses and depositor runs at two institutions in Taiwan Province of China: One institution was taken over by a state-owned bank, and the other supported by the central bank and a state-owned bank. The large state-owned banks are reported to have an overhang of bad loans to real estate projects.

Source: Lindgren et al. (1996), table 2. Sample ends Spring 1996.

Appendix B
Examples of International Standards
in Financial Markets

This appendix describes three earlier international standards in the financial area: the IMF's Special Data Dissemination Standard (SDDS), the G-30's Guidelines for Trading and Settlement of Securities, and the G-30's Guidelines on the Risk Management of Derivatives. Subscription to all three of these initiatives is voluntary.

The IMF's Special Data Dissemination Standard (IMF 1997)

Purpose

The SDDS was established by the IMF to guide members that have, or that might seek, access to international capital markets in the provision of their economic and financial data to the public. The IMF is working towards completion of the General Data Dissemination Standard to guide all its members. Both standards are expected to enhance the availability of timely and comprehensive statistics and therefore contribute to the pursuit of sound macroeconomic policies. The SDDS is also expected to contribute to the improved functioning of financial markets.

Subscription

Subscription to the SDDS was opened in early April 1996 by a letter from the IMF's managing director to all IMF members and governors. Although

**Table B.1 Countries subscribing to the IMF's SDDS, as of
19 February 1997**

Argentina	Australia	Austria
Belgium	Canada	Chile
Colombia	Croatia	Denmark
Finland	France	Germany
Hungary	Iceland	India
Indonesia	Ireland	Israel
Italy	Japan	Malaysia
Latvia	Lithuania	Norway
Mexico	Netherlands	Poland
Peru	Philippines	Slovenia
Singapore	Slovak Republic	South Korea
South Africa	Spain	Sweden
Switzerland	Thailand	Turkey
United Kingdom	United Kingdom (Hong Kong)	United States

Source: Internet http://dsbb.imf.org/overview.htm

subscription is voluntary, it carries a commitment by a subscribing member to observe the standard and to provide certain information to the IMF about its practices in disseminating economic and financial data. A member country's subscription, which can be made at any time, is to be communicated in writing to the secretary of the IMF. To date, there have been 42 subscriptions to the SDDS (see table B.1).

The Dimensions and Monitorable Elements of the Standard

The SDDS, in taking a comprehensive view of the dissemination of economic and financial data, identifies four dimensions of data dissemination:

■ The data: coverage, periodicity, and timeliness;

■ Access by the public;

■ Integrity of the disseminated data; and

■ Quality of the disseminated data.

For each of these dimensions, the SDDS prescribes two to four monitorable elements—good practices that can be observed, or monitored, by the users of statistics.

The data dimension lists 17 data categories that provide coverage for the four sectors of the economy, and it prescribes the periodicity (or frequency) and timeliness with which data for these categories are to be disseminated (see table B.2). In recognition of differences in economic structures and institutional arrangements across countries, the SDDS provides flexibility. Certain categories are marked for dissemination on an "as relevant" basis. Further, some data categories or components of data categories are identified as encouraged rather than prescribed. With respect to periodicity and timeliness, a subscribing member may exercise certain flexibility options while being considered in full observance of the SDDS.

The monitorable elements of the SDDS for access, integrity, and quality emphasize transparency in the compilation and dissemination of statistics.

- To support ready and equal access, the SDDS prescribes (a) advance dissemination of release calendars and (b) simultaneous release to all interested parties.

- To assist users in assessing the integrity of data disseminated under the SDDS, the SDDS prescribes (a) the dissemination of the terms and conditions under which official statistics are produced and disseminated; (b) the identification of internal government access to data before release; (c) the identification of ministerial commentary on the occasion of statistical release; and (d) the provision of information about revision and advance notice of major changes in methodology.

- To assist users in assessing data quality, the SDDS prescribes (a) the dissemination of documentation on statistical methodology and (b) the dissemination of component detail, reconciliations with related data, and statistical frameworks that make possible cross-checks and checks of reasonableness.

Consistent with this comprehensive view of data dissemination, dissemination itself is broadly defined to include electronic dissemination in addition to the more traditional formats.

Transition Period

A transition period for the implementation of the SDDS began with the opening of subscription in early April 1996 and will end on 31 December 1998. During this period a member may subscribe to the SDDS even if its dissemination practices are not fully in line with the SDDS at that time. This period gives subscribers time to adjust their practices, according to a plan that is to be presented and to bring them into line with the standard. During the transition period, the IMF will also elaborate more fully certain operational aspects and review the content and procedures of the SDDS with a view to making any adjustment needed in the light of experience.

Table B.2 IMF special data dissemination standard: coverage, periodicity, and timeliness

Category	Prescribed Components	Encouraged categories and/or components	Periodicity	Timeliness
Real sector				
National accounts; nominal, real, and associated prices *	GDP by major expenditure category and/or by productive sector	Saving, gross national income	Q	Q
Production index/ indices#	Industrial, primary commodity, or sector, as relevant		M (or as relevant)	6W (M encourage or as relevant)
		Forward-looking indicator(s), e.g., qualitative business surveys, orders, composite leading indicators index	M or Q	M or Q
Labor market	Employment, unemployment, and wages/earnings, as relevant		Q	Q
Price indices	Consumer prices and producer or wholesale prices		M	M

Fiscal sector

General government or public sector operations, as relevant*	Revenue, expenditure, balance, and domestic (bank and nonbank) and foreign financing	Interest payments	A	2Q
Central government operations#	Budgetary accounts: revenue, expenditure, balance, and domestic (bank and nonbank) and foreign financing	Interest payments	M	M
Central government debt	Domestic and foreign, as relevant, with a breakdown by currency (including indexed), as relevant, and a breakdown by maturity; debt guaranteed by central government, as relevant	Debt service projections: interest and amortization on medium- and long-term debt (Q for next 4 quarters and then A) and amortization on short-term debt (Q)	Q	Q

(continued next page)

73

Table B.2 (continued)

	Coverage			
	Prescribed			
Category	**Components**	**Encouraged categories and/or components**	**Periodicity**	**Timeliness**
Financial sector				
Analytical accounts of the banking sector*	Money aggregates, domestic credit by public and private sector, external position		M	M
Analytical accounts of the central bank#	Reserve money, domestic claims on public and private sector, external position		M (W encouraged)	2W (W encouraged)
Interest rates	Short- and long-term government security rates, policy-variable rate	Range of representative deposit and lending rates	D	†
Stock market	Share-price index, as relevant		D	†
External sector				
Balance of payments*	Goods and services, net income flows, net current transfers, selected capital (or capital and financial) account items (including reserves)	Foreign direct investment and portfolio investment	Q	Q

Data category	Description	Additional items	Periodicity	Timeliness
International reserves*	Gross official reserves (gold, foreign exchange, SDRs, and IMF position) denominated in US dollars	Reserve-related liabilities, as relevant	M (W encouraged)	W
Merchandise trade#	Exports and imports	Major commodity breakdowns with longer time lapse	M	8W (4-6W encouraged)
International investment position	See accompanying text		A (Q encouraged)	2Q (Q encouraged)
Exchange rates	Spot rates and three- and six-month forward market rates, as relevant		D	†
Addendum: Population		Key distributions, e.g., by age and sex	A	..

Note: Periodicity and timeliness: Daily ("D"); weekly or with lapse of no more than one week after the reference date or close of the reference week ("W"); monthly or with lapse of no more than one month ("M"); quarterly or with lapse of no more than one quarter ("Q"); and annual ("A").

* Comprehensive statistical frameworks

Tracking categories

† Given that data are widely available from private sources, dissemination of official producers may be less time sensitive. Although dissemination by recorded telephone messages or fax services is encouraged, dissemination of these data can be made part of other (preferably high-frequency) dissemination products.

Source: IMF (1996c).

Metadata

A subscriber is expected to submit information about its data and its dissemination practices—its metadata—to the IMF for presentation on the electronic bulletin board. The metadata are to be submitted to the IMF within three months of subscription, except those relating to summary methodologies (for which more time is provided). Subscribers' metadata are reviewed by the IMF for comprehensiveness and international comparability. The responsibility for the accuracy of the metadata, including timely updates, and for the economic and financial data underlying the metadata, rests with the subscriber.

The Role of the Bulletin Board

The Dissemination Standards Bulletin Board (DSBB) will be maintained by the IMF. Metadata are useful in their own right, and their presentation on the DSBB will facilitate monitoring of observance of the standard by the financial markets and other data users. The DSBB will not provide actual data, although ways are being explored to link the DSBB, with its metadata, to actual country data.

A member's presence on the DSBB will indicate that it subscribes to, and intends to observe, certain tenets of good statistical citizenship. Subscribers will not be removed from the DSBB during the transition period except for egregious nonobservance. After the transition period, serious and persistent nonobservance will be caused for removal. Procedures for removal, which could involve a panel of independent experts and would require a decision by the IMF Executive Board, will be elaborated fully during the transition period.

G-30 Guidelines for Trading and Settlement of Securities (G-30 1989)

Recommendation I

By 1990 all comparisons of trades between direct market participants (i.e., brokers, broker/dealers, and other exchange members) should be accomplished by T + 1.[1]

Recommendation II

By 1992 indirect market participants (such as institutional investors or any trading counterparties that are not broker/dealers) should be members of a trade comparison system that achieves positive affirmation of trade details.

---

1. T is the date securities are traded; and T + 1 is 1 day after the trade; and T + 2 is 2 days after the trade.

Recommendation III

Each country should have an effective and fully developed central securities depository, organized and managed to encourage the broadest possible industry participation (directly and indirectly), in place by 1992.

Recommendation IV

Each country should study its market volumes and participation to determine whether a trade-netting system would be beneficial in terms of reducing risk and promoting efficiency. If a netting system would be appropriate, it should be implemented by 1992.

Recommendation V

Delivery versus payment (DVP) should be employed as the method of settling all securities transactions. A DVP system should be in place by 1992.

Recommendation VI

Payments associated with the settlement of securities transactions and the servicing of securities portfolios should be made consistent across all instruments and markets by adopting the "same day" funds convention.

Recommendation VII

A "rolling settlement" system should be adopted by all markets. Final settlement should occur on T + 3 by 1992. As an interim target, final settlement should occur on T + 5 by 1990 at the latest, except where it hinders the achievement of T + 3 by 1992.

Recommendation VIII

Securities lending and borrowing should be encouraged as a method of expediting the settlement of securities transactions. Existing regulatory and taxation barriers that inhibit the practice of lending securities should be removed by 1990.

Recommendation IX

Each country should adopt the standard for securities messages developed by the International Organization of Standardization (IOS Standard 7775). In particular, countries should adopt the ISIN numbering system for securities issues as defined in the ISO Standard 6166, at least for cross-border transactions. These standards should be universally applied by 1992.

Table B.3 shows compliance with these G-30 recommendations for a group of developing countries.

G-30 Guidelines on the Risk Management of Derivatives (G-30 1993)

General Policies

Recommendation 1: The Role of Senior Management

Dealers and end users should use derivatives in a manner consistent with the overall risk management and capital policies approved by their boards of directors. These policies should be reviewed as business and market circumstances change. Policies governing derivatives use should be clearly defined, including the purposes for which these transactions are to be undertaken. Senior management should approve procedures and controls to implement these policies, and management at all levels should enforce them.

Valuation and Market Risk Management

Recommendation 2: Marking to Market

Dealers should mark their derivatives positions to market, on at least a daily basis, for risk management purposes.

Recommendation 3: Market Valuation Methods

Derivatives portfolios of dealers should be valued based on mid-market-levels less specific adjustments, or on appropriate bid or offer levels. Mid-market valuation adjustments should allow for expected future costs such as unearned credit spread, close-out costs, investing and funding costs, and administrative costs.

Recommendation 4: Identifying Revenue Sources

Dealers should measure the components of revenue regularly and in sufficient detail to understand the sources of risk.

Recommendation 5: Measuring Market Risk

Dealers should use a consistent measure to calculate daily the market risk of their derivatives positions and compare it to market risk limits.

Table B.3 Conformity with G-30 recommendations on clearance and settlement of securities

Country	Trade Comparison System (T+1)		Central depositories	Trade netting	Delivery versus payment	Same day funds payment	T+3 rolling settlement	Securities lending
	Direct participants	Indirect participants						
Argentina	Yes		Yes			Yes	Yes	Yes
Brazil	Yes	Yes	Yes	Yes	Yes		Yes	Yes
Chile			Yes		Yes		Yes	
China	Yes	Yes	Yes	Yes		Yes	Yes	Yes
India	Yes			Yes				
Indonesia				Yes	Yes			
Malaysia			Yes	Yes	Yes	Yes		
Mexico	Yes		Yes	Yes	Yes	Yes	Yes	Yes
Pakistan		Yes			Yes	Yes		
Philippines								
Poland			Yes	Yes			Yes	
Russia			Yes					
South Korea	Yes	Yes	Yes	Yes	Yes	Yes	Yes	
Sri Lanka	Yes		Yes	Yes			Yes	
Thailand	Yes		Yes	Yes	Yes		Yes	
Turkey	Yes		Yes	Yes	Yes	Yes		

Source: World Bank (1997).

- Market risk is best measured as "value at risk" using probability analysis based upon a common confidence interval (e.g., two standard deviations) and time horizon (e.g., a one-day exposure).

- Components of market risk that should be considered across the term structure include: absolute price or rate change (delta), convexity (gamma), volatility (vega), time decay (theta), basis or correlation, and discount rate (rho).

Recommendation 6: Stress Simulations

Dealers should regularly perform simulations to determine how their portfolios would perform under stress conditions.

Recommendation 7: Investing and Funding Forecasts

Dealers should periodically forecast the cash investing and funding requirements arising from their derivatives portfolios.

Recommendation 8: Independent Market Risk Management

Dealers should have a market risk management function, with clear independence and authority, to ensure that the following responsibilities are carried out:

- The development of risk limit policies and the monitoring of transactions and positions for adherence to these policies. (See Recommendation 5.)

- The design of stress scenarios to measure the impact of market conditions, however improbable, that might cause market gaps, volatility swings, or disruptions of major relationships, or might reduce liquidity in the face of unfavorable market linkages, concentrated market making, or credit exhaustion. (See Recommendation 6.)

- The design of revenue reports quantifying the contribution of various risk components and of market risk measures such as value at risk. (See Recommendations 4 and 5.)

- The monitoring of variance between the actual volatility of portfolio value and that predicted by the measure of market risk.

- The review and approval of pricing models and valuation systems used by front- and back-office personnel and the development of reconciliation procedures if different systems are used.

Recommendation 9: Practices by End Users

As appropriate to the nature, size, and complexity of their derivatives activities, end users should adopt the same valuation and market risk management practices that are recommended for dealers. Specifically, they should consider: regularly marking to market their derivatives transactions for risk management purposes; periodically forecasting the cash investing and funding requirements arising from their derivatives transactions; and establishing a clearly independent and authoritative function to design and assure adherence to prudent risk limits.

Credit Risk Measurement and Management

Recommendation 10: Measuring Credit Exposure

Dealers and end users should measure credit exposure on derivatives in two ways:

- Current exposure, which is the replacement cost of derivatives transactions—that is, their market value.

- Potential exposure, which is an estimate of the future replacement cost of derivatives transactions. It should be calculated using probability analysis based upon broad confidence intervals (e.g., two-standard deviations) over the remaining terms of the transactions.

Recommendation 11: Aggregating Credit Exposures

Credit exposures on derivatives, and all other credit exposures to a counterparty, should be aggregated taking into consideration enforceable netting arrangements. Credit exposures should be calculated regularly and compared to credit limits.

Recommendation 12: Independent Credit Risk Management

Dealers and end users should have a credit risk management function with clear independence and authority, and with analytical capabilities in derivatives, responsible for:

- Approving credit exposure measurement standards.

- Setting credit limits and monitoring their use.

- Reviewing credits and concentrations of credit risk.

- Reviewing and monitoring risk reduction arrangements.

Recommendation 13: Master Agreements

Dealers and end users are encouraged to use one master agreement as widely as possible with each counterparty to document existing and future derivatives transactions, including foreign exchange forwards and options. Master agreements should provide for payments netting and close-out netting, using a full two-way payments approach.

Recommendation 14: Credit Enhancement

Dealers and end users should assess both the benefits and costs of credit enhancement and related risk-reduction arrangements. Where it is proposed that credit down-grades would trigger early termination or collateral requirements, participants should carefully consider their own capacity and that of their counterparties to meet the potentially substantial funding needs that might result.

Enforceability

Recommendation 15: Promoting Enforceability

Dealers and end users should work together on a continuing basis to identify and recommend solutions for issues of legal enforceability, both within and across jurisdictions, as activities evolve and new types of transactions are developed.

Systems, Operations, and Controls

Recommendation 16: Professional Expertise

Dealers and end users must ensure that their derivatives activities are undertaken by professionals in sufficient number and with the appropriate experience, skill levels, and degrees of specialization. These professionals include specialists who transact and manage the risks involved, their supervisors, and those responsible for processing, reporting, controlling, and auditing the activities.

Recommendation 17: Systems

Dealers and end users must ensure that adequate systems for data capture, processing, settlement, and management reporting are in place so that derivatives transactions are conducted in an orderly and efficient manner in compliance with management policies. Dealers should have risk management systems that measure the risks incurred in their derivatives activities including market and credit risks. End users should have risk management systems that measure the risks incurred in their derivatives activities based upon their nature, size, and complexity.

Recommendation 18: Authority

Management of dealers and end users should designate who is authorized to commit their institutions to derivatives transactions.

Recommendation 19: Accounting Practices

International harmonization of accounting standards for derivatives is desirable. Pending the adoption of harmonized standards, the following accounting practices are recommended:

■ Dealers should account for derivatives transactions by marking them to market and taking changes in value to income each period.

■ End users should account for derivatives used to manage risks so as to achieve a consistency of income recognition treatment between those instruments and the risks being managed. Thus, if the risk being managed is accounted for at cost (or, in the case of an anticipatory hedge, not yet recognized), changes in the value of a qualifying risk management instrument should be deferred until a gain or loss is recognized on the risk being managed. Or, if the risk being managed is market to market with changes in value being taken to income, a qualifying risk management instrument should be treated in a comparable fashion.

■ End users should account for derivatives not qualifying for risk management treatment on a mark-to-market basis.

■ Amounts due to and from counterparties should only be offset when there is a legal right to set off or when enforceable netting arrangements are in place.

Where local regulations prevent adoption of these practices, disclosure along these lines is nevertheless recommended.

Recommendation 20: Disclosures

Financial statements of dealers and end users should contain sufficient information about their use of derivatives to provide an understanding of the purposes for which transactions are undertaken, the extent of the transactions, the degree of risk involved, and how the transactions have been accounted for. Pending the adoption of harmonized accounting standards, the following disclosures are recommended:

■ Information about management's attitude to financial risks, how instruments are used, and how risks are monitored and controlled.

■ Accounting policies.

■ Analysis of positions at the balance-sheet date.

■ Analysis of the credit risk inherent in those positions.

■ For dealers only, additional information about the extent of their activities in financial instruments.

Recommendations for Legislators, Regulators, and Supervisors

Recommendation 21: Recognizing Netting

Regulators and supervisors should recognize the benefits of netting arrangements where and to the full extent that they are enforceable and encourage their use by reflecting these arrangements in capital adequacy standards. Specifically, they should promptly implement the recognition of the effectiveness of bilateral close-out netting in bank capital regulations.

Recommendation 22: Legal and Regulatory Uncertainties

Legislators, regulators, and supervisors, including central banks, should work in concert with dealers and end users to identify and remove any remaining legal and regulatory uncertainties with respect to:

- The form of documentation required to create legally enforceable agreements (statute of frauds).

- The capacity of parties, such as governmental entities, insurance companies, pension funds, and building societies, to enter into transactions (ultra vires).

- The enforceability of bilateral close-out netting and collateral arrangements in bankruptcy.

- The enforceability of multibranch netting arrangements in bankruptcy.

- The legality/enforceability of derivatives transactions.

Recommendation 23: Tax Treatment

Legislators and tax authorities are encouraged to review and, where appropriate, amend tax laws and regulations that disadvantage the use of derivatives in risk management strategies. Tax impediments include the inconsistent or uncertain tax treatment of gains and losses on the derivatives, in comparison with the gains and losses that arise from the risks being managed.

Recommendation 24: Accounting Standards

Accounting standards-setting bodies in each country should, as a matter of priority, provide comprehensive guidance on accounting and reporting of transactions in financial instruments, including derivatives, and should work towards international harmonization of standards on this subject. Also, the International Accounting Standards Committee should finalize its accounting standard on financial instruments.

Appendix C
Banking Activities, Bank Ownership, and Commercial Bank Supervisory Practices in EU and G-10 Countries, 1995

Table C.1 Permissible banking activities and bank ownership in EU and G-10 countries, 1995

Country	Securities[a]	Insurance[b]	Real estate[c]	Commercial bank investment in nonfinancial firms	Nonfinancial firm investment in commercial banks	Geographic branching restrictions
Austria	Unrestricted	Permitted	Unrestricted	Unrestricted	Unrestricted	None
Belgium	Permitted	Permitted	Restricted	Restricted	Unrestricted	None
Canada	Permitted	Permitted	Permitted	Restricted	Restricted	None
Denmark	Unrestricted	Permitted	Permitted	Permitted	Unrestricted	None
Finland	Unrestricted	Restricted	Permitted	Unrestricted	Unrestricted	None
France	Unrestricted	Permitted	Permitted	Unrestricted	Unrestricted	None
Germany	Unrestricted	Restricted	Permitted	Unrestricted	Unrestricted	None
Greece	Permitted	Restricted	Restricted	Unrestricted	Unrestricted	None
Ireland	Unrestricted	Prohibited	Unrestricted	Unrestricted	Unrestricted	None
Italy	Unrestricted	Permitted	Restricted	Restricted	Restricted	None
Japan	Restricted	Prohibited	Restricted	Restricted	Restricted	None
Luxembourg	Unrestricted	Permitted	Unrestricted	Unrestricted	Restricted	None
Netherlands	Unrestricted	Permitted	Permitted	Unrestricted	Unrestricted	None
Portugal	Unrestricted	Permitted	Restricted	Permitted	Unrestricted	None
Spain	Unrestricted	Permitted	Restricted	Unrestricted	Permitted	None
Sweden	Unrestricted	Permitted	Restricted	Restricted	Restricted	None
Switzerland	Unrestricted	Permitted	Unrestricted	Unrestricted	Unrestricted	None
United Kingdom	Unrestricted	Permitted	Unrestricted	Unrestricted	Unrestricted	None
United States	Restricted	Restricted	Restricted	Restricted	Restricted	Yes[d]

Note: Unrestricted: a full range of activities in the given category can be conducted directly in the bank.
Permitted: a full range of activities can be conducted, but all or some must be conducted in subsidiaries.
Restricted: less than a full range of activities can be conducted in the bank or subsidiaries.
Prohibited: the activity cannot be conducted in either the bank or subsidiaries.

a. Securities activities include underwriting, dealing and brokering all kinds of securities, and all aspects of the mutual fund business.
b. Insurance activities include underwriting and selling insurance products/services as principal or agent.
c. Real estate activities include investment, development, and management.
d. Will be largely eliminated in late 1997 as the Riegle-Neal Interstate Banking Act takes effect.

Source: Barth et al. (1996).

Table C.2 Commercial bank supervisory practices in EU and G-10 countries: 1995

	Austria	Belgium	Denmark	Finland	France	Germany	Greece	Ireland	Italy	Luxembourg
Components of capital for meeting the capital standard or requirements										
Noncumulative perpetual preferred stock	Yes	Yes	No, does not exist	Yes	No, issues not permitted in domestic market	Yes	Yes	Yes, no limits	Yes, but limits	Yes
Current year profit-added (or loss deducted)	Yes	Yes	Yes	Yes	Yes	No	Yes	Yes	Yes	Yes
Intangible assets other than goodwill	No	No	No	No	No, except for lease renewal rights	No	Yes	No	Yes	No
Goodwill[a]	No	No	No	No	No	No	Yes	No	Yes	No
Undisclosed reserves[b]	Yes, but limits	Yes, but limits	No information	No	No	Yes, but limits	No	No	No	Yes
Hybrid capital instruments (including cumulative perpetual preferred stock)[c]	Yes, but limits	Yes, but limits	No, does not exist	Yes	Yes	Yes, but limits	Yes, but limits	Yes, but limits	Yes, but limits	Yes
Subordinated term debt[d]	Yes, but limits	Yes, but limits	Yes	Yes	Yes	Yes, but limits	Yes, but limits	Yes, but limits	Yes, but limits	Yes
Limited life redeemable preference shares[e]	No	Yes, but limits	No, does not exist	Not applicable	Yes, but not issued	No	Yes, but not utilized at present	Yes, but limits	No, does not exist	Yes

Fixed asset revaluation reserves[f]	No	No, does not exist	Yes	Yes	No	Yes, but limits	Yes, but limits	Yes, but limits	No
Latent or hidden revaluation reserves[g]	No	No, does not exist	No	No	Yes, but limits	No	No	No	Yes
General loan-loss reserves[h]	Yes	No, does not exist	Yes	Yes	Yes, but limits	Yes	Yes, but limits	Yes, but limits	Yes
Investment in the capital of other banks and financial institutions	No	No	No	Yes, but limits	No	No	No	No	No
Examinations and/or inspections									
On-site	Yes	Yes, usually every 3 years	Yes, not regularly	Yes	Yes	Yes, generally every 2-3 years	Yes, usually every 18-24 months	Yes, usually every 4-8 years	Yes, ad hoc basis
Banks pay exam	No	Yes	Yes	No information	Yes	No	No	No	Yes
External audits									
Required external audits	Yes	Yes	Yes	Yes	Yes	Yes	Yes	Yes, for banks quoted on the stock exchange	Yes

(continued next page, see page 96 for notes)

Table C.2 Commercial bank supervisory practices in EU and G-10 countries: 1995 (continued)

	Austria	Belgium	Denmark	Finland	France	Germany	Greece	Ireland	Italy	Luxembourg
Information publicly disclosed										
Bank examinations or inspections	No	No	No	No	No information	No	No	No	No	No
Enforcement actions	No	Yes	No	No	No information	No	No	No	Yes	No
Consumer protection laws										
Consumer protection laws exist	Yes	Yes	No, not specifically for banks	Yes	No information	Yes	Yes	Yes	Yes	Yes
Domestic bank activities abroad										
Specific authorization required	No	No, only notification	No	No	No	No	Yes	Yes	Yes	No
Limits or restrictions placed on domestic banks' foreign activities	No	No, only notification	No	No	No	No	No	No	No	No
Rates paid on deposits or charged on loans										
Restrictions or controls	No	Yes, only on consumer loans and special savings accounts	No	Yes	No information	No	No	No	No	No

(continued next page, see page 96 for notes)

Lending limits on											
Single borrower	Yes	Yes	Yes	Yes	Yes	No information	Yes	Yes	Yes	Yes	Yes
Persons connected with the bank	Yes	Yes	No	No	Yes	No information	Yes	No	No	Yes	Yes
Particular sectors	No	No	No	No	No	No information	Yes	No	No	No	No
Country risk exposure	No	No	No	No	No	No information	Yes	No	No	No	No
Large exposures	Yes	Yes	Yes	Yes	Yes	No information	Yes	Yes	No	Yes	Yes

Table C.2 Commercial bank supervisory practices in EU and G-10 countries: 1995 (continued)

	Netherlands	Portugal	Spain	Sweden	United Kingdom	Canada	Japan	Switzerland	United States
Noncumulative perpetual preferred stock	Yes	Yes	Yes	Yes	Yes	Yes	Yes	Yes, no limits	Yes
Current year profit-added (or loss deducted)	Yes	Yes	No	Yes	Yes	Yes	Yes	Yes	Yes
Intangible assets other than goodwill	Yes	Yes	No	No	No	Yes	Yes	No	No, with limited exceptions
Goodwill[a]	Yes	Yes	No	No	No	No	No	No	No
Undisclosed reserves[b]	Yes	No information	No	No	Not applicable	No	No	Yes, but limits	No
Hybrid capital instruments (including cumulative perpetual preferred stock)[c]	Yes	Yes	Yes, but limits	Yes, with approval	Yes, but limits	Yes	Yes, but not prevalent	No, not including cumulative perpetual preferred stock	Yes, but limits
Subordinated term debt[d]	Yes	Yes, but limits	Yes, but limits	Yes	Yes, but limits	Yes	Yes	Yes, but limits	Yes, but limits
Limited life redeemable preference shares[e]	Yes	No information	Yes, but limits	No	Yes	Yes	Yes, but not issues	No	Yes, but limits
Fixed asset revaluation reserves[f]	Yes	Yes	Yes, but limits	Yes, with approval	Yes, with caution	No	No	Yes, but limits	No

Latent or hidden revaluation reserves[g]	Yes	No information	No	No	No	Yes	Yes, but limits	No
General loan-loss reserves[h]	Yes	Yes	No	Not applicable	No	Yes	Yes, no limits	Yes, but limits
Investment in the capital of other banks and financial institutions	Yes	No	No	No	Yes, but back to back issues are deducted	No, if sole purpose is to raise capital ration	No	No
Examinations and/or inspections								
On-Site	Yes, depends of size/risk profile	Yes, usually annually	Yes	Yes, but limited and usually biennially	Yes, annually	Yes	Yes, every year	Yes
Banks pay exam	No	No	No	No, not directly	Yes	No information	Yes	Yes
External audits								
Required external audits	Yes	Yes	Yes	Yes	Yes	No information	Yes, official part of supervisory system	Yes, for banks with assets exceeding $500 million

(continued next page, see page 96 for notes)

Table C.2 Commercial bank supervisory practices in EU and G-10 countries: 1995 (continued)

	Netherlands	Portugal	Spain	Sweden	United Kingdom	Canada	Japan	Switzerland	United States
Information publicly disclosed									
Bank examinations or inspections	No	No	No	No	No	No	No information	No	No
Enforcement actions	No	Yes	No	No	Yes, but not explicitly naming institutions	No	No information	No	Yes
Consumer protection laws									
Consumer protection laws exist	Yes	Yes	Yes	Yes	No	Yes	No information	No	Yes
Domestic bank activities abroad									
Specific authorization required	No	Yes	Yes, but only branches outside EU	No	No	No^j	No information	No, only notification	No
Limits or restrictions places on domestic banks' foreign activities	Yes	No	No	No	No	No^j	No information	No	Yes

Rates paid on deposits or charged on loans							
Restrictions of controls	No	No	No	No	No	No, with few relatively minor exceptions	Yes, only on loans	Yes, but not particularly confining
Lending limits on								
Single borrower	Yes	Yes	Yes	Yes	Yes	Yes	Yes	Yes
Persons connected with the bank	Yes	Yes	No	Yes[l]	Yes	No information	Yes	Yes
Particular sectors	Yes	No	Yes	Yes[l]	No	No information	Yes	No
Country risk exposure	Yes	No	No	Yes[l]	No	No information	No, but provision requirements per country	No
Large exposures	Yes	Yes	Yes	Yes[l]	Yes	No information	Yes	No

(continued next page, see page 96 for notes)

a. Goodwill is an intangible asset.

b. Undisclosed reserves are portions of accumulated after-tax retained earnings not identified in the published balance sheet or otherwise disclosed, except to banking supervisors.

c. Hybrid-capital instruments including cumulative preferred stock are instruments that combine the characteristics of equity capital and debt and should meet the following requirements: unsecured, subordinated, and fully paid-up; not redeemable at the initiative of the holder or without prior consent of supervisory authority; available to participate in losses without the bank being obliged to cease trading (unlike conventional subordinated debt); and all service obligations to be deferred where the profitability of the bank would not support payment.

d. Subordinated term debt is normally not available to participate in losses of a bank that continues operating (included in capital only if minimum maturity of five years).

e. Limited life redeemable preference shares are the same as immediately before.

f. Fixed asset revaluation reserves represent a formal revaluation—carried through to the balance sheet—of a bank's own premises.

g. Latent or hidden revaluation reserves are the difference between the market value and historic cost book value of long-term holdings of equity securities.

h. General loan-loss reserves are reserves that are held against future and presently unidentified losses and are freely available to meet losses that may subsequently materialize.

i. Explicitly or implicitly, in relation to the size of the bank's capital base.

j. Depends on nature and circumstances of the bank and country involved.

Note: The Basle Committee on Banking Supervision (composed of representatives of the central banks and supervisory authorities from the G-10 countries and Luxembourg) adopted the Basle Accord in July 1988. The Basle Accord is noncompulsory and applies only to internationally active banks. It is composed of four basic elements: (1) an agreed upon definition of tier 1 (or core) capital, consisting primarily of common stockholders' equity and noncumulative perpetual preferred stock; (2) additional components of capital, constituting tier 2 capital; (3) a general framework for assigning assets and off-balance-sheet items to broad risk categories and procedures for calculating risk-based categories and procedures for calculating a risk-based capital ratio; and (4) a schedule for achieving, by no later than the end of 1992, a minimum ratio of total capital (tier 1 plus tier 2) to risk-weighted assets of 8 percent (of which at least 4 percent should be in the form of core capital).

The European Union issued two directives primarily addressing capital standards: the Own Funds and Solvency Ratio Directives, which were adopted in April 1989 and December 1989, respectively. These directives have the force of law and apply to all banks incorporated in the member state. Banks were required to meet a minimum 8 percent risk-weighted capital ratio by 1 January 1993. The EU directives refer to "original own funds" and "additional own funds" rather than to tier 1 (core) capital and tier 2 (supplemental) capital. However, these differences in terminology have no substantive effect.

The Basle Accord and the EU directives do not provide for identical minimum capital standards for banks.

Sources: Supervisory authorities in the listed countries provided information used to prepare this table. However, they are not responsible for any errors or misinterpretations. For exact information, one must consult the pertinent laws and regulations in the individual countries. *The Capital Equivalency Report,* US Board of Governors of the Federal Reserve System and US Secretary of the Department of the Treasury, 19 June 1992, was a source for France and Japan. Also, in the case of France, a source was *Bank Regulatory Structure: France,* US General Accounting Office, August 1995.

Appendix D
Two Examples of Disclosure of the Financial Condition of Banks

Aggregate Positions: Data for National Banks in the United States (Goldstein and Turner 1996)

Table D.1

Income	Balance sheet	Performance ratios
Net income	Assets	Return on equity
Net interest income	Loans	Return on assets
Noninterest income	Real estate	Net interest margin
Noninterest expense	Commercial and industrial	
Loan-loss provision	Noncurrent loans[a]	Loss provisions to loans
Gains on securities sales, net	Other real estate owned	Net loan loss to loans
Extraordinary income	Securities not trading	Noncurrent loans to loans
Net loan loss		Loss reserves to loans
	Total liabilities	Loss reserves to noncurrent loans
	Total deposits	
	Domestic deposits	Loans to assets
	Loan-loss reserve	Loans to deposits
		Equity to assets
	Equity capital	Estimated leverage ratio[b]
	Total capital	Estimated risk-based capital ratio

Note: These aggregate data cover around 3,000 banks and are published quarterly.

a. Sum of loans and leases 90 days or more past due, plus loans not earning the contractual rate of interest in the loan agreement.

b. Ratio of estimated tier 1 capital to estimated tangible total assets.

Source: Office of the Comptroller of the Currency, *Quarterly Journal*

Individual Positions: New Zealand's New Disclosure Regime For Banks (Mortlock 1996; Nicholl 1996)

The aim of bank supervision in New Zealand is to maintain a sound and efficient financial system. The protection of depositors is not an aim in itself; there is no deposit insurance.

Registration of Banks

Bank registration entitles the institution to use the word "bank" in its name; but registration is not required to conduct banking business.[1] The Reserve Bank of New Zealand is responsible for deciding on applications for bank registration subject to certain conditions:

- Total capital of at least 8 percent of the banking group's risk-weighted credit exposures, of which at least one-half must be tier 1 capital.[2]

- Group's credit exposure to major shareholders and related entities not permitted to exceed: (a) 15 percent of tier 1 capital in the case of lending to a nonbank and (b) 75 percent of tier 1 capital in the case of lending to a bank.

- Locally incorporated banks to have at least two independent directors and a nonexecutive chairman.

Reserve Bank Action When a Bank's Capital Falls Below Requirements

Recent reforms introduced a more structured approach with the aim of reducing the scope for regulatory forbearance by the banking supervisor.

- If a bank's tier 1 or total capital falls below the limits noted above, the bank would have to submit to the Reserve Bank a plan for restoring capital, including the following elements: (a) no dividends paid until the minimum capital requirements have been compiled with; (b) no increase in exposure to related parties from the level prevailing when

---

1. However, compliance with disclosure and other requirements contained in the Securities Act is required.

2. At the time of announcement, the Reserve Bank noted, "Although the Bank considers that disclosure alone, without minimum requirements, should provide sufficient incentives for banks to at least adhere to the international norm of 8 percent, it believes the retention of the capital requirement offers benefits in terms of international credibility, at little, if any, marginal costs to banks."

capital requirements first breached; and (c) if reduction in capital results in a bank being in breach of the limit on related party exposures, the bank would be required to reduce its exposure to a level that complies with the limit.

- If a bank's tier 1 capital fall below 3 percent of risk-weighted exposures, gross credit exposures must not be increased from the level which occurred when capital first fell below this limit.

- The plan would be published in the bank's public disclosure statement at the first practicable opportunity.

Form of Disclosure

- Quarterly, with two main—forms, one brief ("Key Information Summary") and the other longer ("General Disclosure Statement"). A Supplemental Disclosure Statement discloses details of any guarantee arrangements and conditions of registration imposed by the Reserve Bank.

- At the half-year and end-of-year, disclosure statements must be published not later than three months after the relevant balance date. In the first and third quarters of a bank's financial year, banks have only two months to publish the disclosure statements, given that in these quarters the disclosure statements are of an abbreviated nature.

Key Information Summary

This one- or two-page note must be displayed prominently in every bank branch and include:

- *Credit rating.* If the bank has one, it must disclose the credit rating given to its long-term senior unsecured liabilities payable in New Zealand. It must also disclose the name of the rating agency, any qualifications (e.g., "credit watch" status), and any changes made in the two years preceding the balance date. A bank with no credit rating must disclose prominently that fact.[3]

- *Capital adequacy.* Risk-weighted capital ratios, as measured using Basle capital requirements.

- *Impaired assets.* Amount and specific provisions held against them.

---

3. The initial intention of imposing a mandatory rating on all banks was abandoned in the face of opposition from smaller banks that argued that this would impose unnecessary costs on them.

- *Exposure concentration.* Disclosed when it exceeds 10 percent of group's equity; disclosure is based on group's peak lending to individual customers over the accounting period. Disclosed as the number of exposures between 10 percent and 20 percent of the group's equity, the number between 20 percent and 30 percent and so on.

- *Connected lending.* Amount of credit exposure to connected persons, based on peak exposure over the accounting period.

- *Profitability* and statement as to *whether liabilities are guaranteed* by another party.

General Disclosure Statement

Contains all the information in the Key Information Summary but in greater detail and additional information such as:

- *Capital and exposure information.* Detailed information on tier 1 and tier 2 capital and credit exposure (both on- and off-balance-sheet) for the bank and the banking group.

- *Funds management.* Information on securitization, unit trusts, superannuation funds, and other fiduciary activities. Explanation of measures in place to minimize risks that might affect the banking group's balance sheet.

- *Sectoral information.* Credit exposure by industry sectors and geographical areas. Main sources of funds by geographical area, by product, and by counterparty type.

- *Risk management systems.* Description of internal audit function and extent to which systems are subject to review.

- *Market risk exposures.* Banking group's exposure to changes in interest rates, foreign exchange rates, and equity prices. Market risk disclosure is for the bank's whole book (both the banking book and the trading book). These disclosure requirements give banks the option of calculating interest rate risk using the Reserve Bank model (based on the Basle market risk model) or using their own model, provided that it produces a result that is at least as conservative as the Reserve Bank model. Both peak and end-of-period exposures must be disclosed.

- Detailed information on *asset quality* and *credit exposure concentration.*

Directors' Attestations and Legal Responsibilities

Every disclosure statement must contain attestations signed by every director of the bank. The attestations relate to:

- Whether the bank has adequate systems in place to monitor and manage the banking group's business risks (including credit risk, concentration risk, equity risk, foreign exchange risk, interest rate risk, and liquidity risk) and whether those systems are being properly applied;

- Whether the banking group's exposures to related parties are contrary to the interest of the banking group;

- Whether the bank is complying with its conditions of registration; and

- That the disclosure statement is not false or misleading.

Directors face serious criminal and civil penalties (including imprisonment, fines, and unlimited personal liability for depositors' losses) for false or misleading statements. Directors may also incur common law liability if they allow the bank to continue to accept funds on the basis of a disclosure statement that, although not false or misleading when signed, has become false or misleading as a result of subsequent material adverse developments.

Reserve Bank's Responsibilities

Under the disclosure framework, the Reserve Bank:

- Will monitor banks' disclosure statements to maintain a sound understanding of the financial condition of the banking system.

- Will monitor banks' compliance with disclosure requirements and conditions of registration. The Reserve Bank also has the power to require a bank to correct and republish a disclosure statement found to be false or misleading.

- Can initiate legal proceedings against a bank and its directors if a statement is thought to be false or misleading.

The Reserve Bank retains extensive crisis management powers under its act, including the powers to appoint an investigator, give directives to a bank and recommend that a bank be placed under statutory management.

References

Akerlof, George. 1970. "The Market for Lemons: Quality Uncertainty and the Market Mechanism." *Quarterly Journal of Economics* 84, no. 3 (August): 488-500.

Avery, Robert, Terrence Belton, and Michael Goldberg. 1988. "Market Discipline in Regulating Bank Risk: New Evidence from the Capital Markets." *Journal of Money, Credit, and Banking* 20, no. 4 (November): 597-610.

Bank for International Settlements (BIS). 1995. *65th Annual Report.* Basle: Bank for International Settlements.

Bank for International Settlements (BIS). 1996. *66th Annual Report.* Basle: Bank for International Settlements.

Barth, James, Daniel Nolle, and Tara Rice. 1996. "Commercial Banking Structure, Regulation, and Performance: An International Comparison." Draft Working Paper. Washington: Office of the Comptroller of the Currency (September).

Basle Committee on Banking Supervision. 1996. *Report on International Developments in Banking Supervision.* Report No. 10. Basle: Basle Committee on Banking Supervision.

Benston, George. 1973. "Bank Examination." *The Bulletin,* no. 89-90. New York: NYU Center for the Study of Financial Institutions (May).

Benston, George, and George Kaufman. 1988. *Risk and Solvency Regulation of Depository Institutions: Past Policies and Current Options.* Monograph Series in Finance and Economics. New York: New York University Press.

Benston, George, and George Kaufman. 1996. "FDICIA after Five Years: A Review and Evaluation." Paper presented at the Brookings Conference on FDICIA: Bank Reform Five Years Later and Five Years Ahead, 19 December, Washington. Forthcoming in *Journal of Economic Perspectives.*

Bergsten, C. Fred, and C. Randall Henning. 1996. *Global Economic Leadership and the Group of Seven.* Washington: Institute for International Economics.

Bernanke, Ben. 1983. "Non-monetary Effects of the Financial Crisis in the Propagation of the Great Depression." *American Economic Review* 73, no. 3 (June): 257-76.

Calomiris, Charles. 1996. "Building an Incentive-Compatible Safety Net: Special Problems for Developing Countries." Unpublished. New York: Columbia University Graduate School of Business.

Calomiris, Charles, and Eugene White. 1994. "The Origins of Federal Deposit Insurance." In Claudia Goldin and Gary Libecap, *The Regulated Economy*. Chicago: University of Chicago Press.

Calvo, Guillermo, and Morris Goldstein. 1996. "Crisis Prevention and Crisis Management after Mexico: What Role for the Official Sector?" In Guillermo Calvo, Morris Goldstein, and Eduard Hochreiter, *Private Capital Flows to Emerging Markets After the Mexican Crisis*. Washington: Institute for International Economics.

Calvo, Guillermo, Leonardo Leiderman, and Carmen Reinhart. 1993. "Capital Inflows and Real Exchange Rate Appreciation in Latin America: The Role of External Factors." *IMF Staff Papers* 40, no. 1 (March): 108-50.

Calvo, Sara, and Carmen Reinhart. 1996. "Capital Flows to Latin America: Is There Evidence of Contagion Effects?" In Guillermo Calvo, Morris Goldstein, and Eduard Hochreiter, *Private Capital Flows to Emerging Markets After the Mexican Crisis*. Washington: Institute for International Economics.

Camdessus, Michel. 1996. "Promoting Safe and Sound Banking Systems: An IMF Perspective." Presentation at the IDB Conference on Safe and Sound Financial Systems: What Works for Latin America, 28 September, Washington.

Caprio, Gerard, and Daniela Klingebiel. 1996a. "Bank Insolvencies: Cross-Country Experience." Unpublished. Washington: World Bank.

Caprio, Gerard, and Daniela Klingebiel. 1996b. "Bank Insolvency: Bad Luck, Bad Policy, or Bad Banking?" In Michael Bruno and and Boris Pleskovic, *Annual World Bank Conference on Development Economics*. Washington: World Bank.

Caprio, Gerard, Izak Atiyas, and James Hanson. 1994. *Financial Reform: Theory and Experience*. Cambridge, UK: Cambridge University Press.

Cline, William. 1995. *International Debt Reexamined*. Washington: Institute for International Economics.

De Gregorio, Jose, and Pablo Guidotti. 1992. *Financial Development and Economic Growth*. IMF Working Paper No. 92/101. Washington: International Monetary Fund.

De Juan, Aristobulo. 1996. "The Roots of Banking Crises: Microeconomic Issues and Regulation and Supervision." In Ricardo Hausman and Liliana Rojas-Suarez, *Banking Crises in Latin America*. Washington: Inter-American Development Bank and Johns Hopkins Press.

Dermine, Jean. 1996. "International Trade in Banking." In Claude Barfield, *International Financial Markets: Harmonization versus Competition*. Washington: American Enterprise Institute.

Dooley, Michael, Eduardo Fernandez-Arias, and Kenneth Kletzer. 1994. *Recent Private Capital Inflows to Developing Countries: Is the Debt Crisis History?* NBER Working Paper No. 4792. Cambridge, MA: National Bureau of Economic Research.

Dziobek, Claudia, Olivier Frecaut, and Maria Nieto. 1995. *Non-G-10 Countries and the Basle Capital Rules: How Tough a Challenge Is It to Join the Basle Club?* IMF Paper on Policy Analysis and Assessment (PPAA) No. 95/5. Washington: International Monetary Fund.

Edwards, Sebastian. 1995. "Public-Sector Deficits and Macroeconomic Stability in Developing Countries." In *Budget Deficits and Debt: Issues and Options*. Kansas City: Federal Reserve Bank of Kansas City.

Federal Deposit Insurance Corporation (FDIC). 1996. "History of the 1980s: Lessons for the Future: Summary." Washington: Federal Deposit Insurance Corporation.

Fernandez, Roque. 1996. "Capital Flows and the Liquidity Shock." In Guillermo Calvo, Morris Goldstein, and Eduard Hochreiter *Private Capital Flows to Emerging Economies After the Mexican Crisis*. Washington: Institute for International Economics.

Financial Action Task Force on Money Laundering. 1990. *Report*. Paris (February).

Flannery, Mark, and Sorin Sorescu. 1996. "Evidence of Bank Market Discipline in the Subordinated Debenture Yields: 1983-1991." *Journal of Finance* 51, no. 4 (September): 1347-78.

Folkerts-Landau, David, Garry Schinasi, Marcel Cassard, Victor Ng, Carmen Reinhart, and Michael Spencer. 1995. "Effects of Capital Flows on the Domestic Financial Sectors in APEC Developing Countries." In Mohsin Khan and Carmen Reinhart, *Capital Flows in the APEC Region*. IMF Occasional Paper No. 122. Washington: International Monetary Fund.

Frenkel, Jacob, Morris Goldstein, and Paul Masson. 1990. "The Rationale for, and Effects of, International Economic Policy Coordination." In William Branson, Jacob Frenkel, and Morris Goldstein, *International Policy Coordination and Exchange Rate Fluctuations*. Chicago: National Bureau of Economic Research and University of Chicago Press.

Garber, Peter. 1996. "Managing Risks to Financial Markets from Volatile Capital Flows: The Role of Prudential Regulation." *International Journal of Finance and Economics* 1, no. 3: 188-95.

Gavin, Michael, and Ricardo Hausman. 1996a. "The Roots of Banking Crises: The Macroeconomic Context." In Ricardo Hausman and Liliana Rojas-Suarez, *Banking Crises in Latin America*. Washington: Inter-American Development Bank and Johns Hopkins University Press.

Gavin, Michael, and Ricardo Hausman. 1996b. "Make or Buy: Approaches to Financial Market Integration." Paper presented at the IDB Conference on Safe and Sound Financial Systems: What Works for Latin America, 27-28 September, Washington.

Goldstein, Morris. 1995a. *The Exchange Rate System and the IMF: A Modest Agenda*, POLICY ANALYSES IN INTERNATIONAL ECONOMICS 39. Washington: Institute for International Economics.

Goldstein, Morris. 1995b. "International Financial Markets and Systemic Risk." Unpublished. Washington: Institute for International Economics.

Goldstein, Morris. 1996a. "The Case for an International Banking Standard." Unpublished. Washington: Institute for International Economics.

Goldstein, Morris. 1996b. "From Halifax to Lyons: What Has Been Done about Crisis Management?" *Essays in International Finance No. 200*. Princeton, NJ: Princeton University, International Finance Section, Economics Department.

Goldstein, Morris, and Philip Turner. 1996. *Banking Crises in Emerging Economies: Origins and Policy Options*. BIS Economic Paper No. 46. Basle: Bank for International Settlements.

Goldstein, Morris, David Folkerts-Landau, Steven Fries, Peter Garber, Tim Lane, Liliana Rojas-Suarez, Michael Spencer, Charles Collyns, Robert Rennhack, and Philippe Szymczak. 1993. *International Capital Markets: Part II. Systemic Issues in International Finance*. IMF World Economic and Financial Surveys. Washington: International Monetary Fund.

Gorton, Gary, and Anthony Santomero. 1990. "Market Discipline and Bank Subordinated Debt." *Journal of Money, Credit, and Banking* 22, no. 1 (February); 119-28.

Group of Seven (G-7). 1996. "Lyon Summit Economic Communiqué: Making a Success of Globalization for the Benefit of All." Statement to the press following the G-7 meeting, 28 June, Lyon.

Group of Ten (G-10). 1996. *The Resolution of Sovereign Liquidity Crises: A Report to the Ministers and Governors under the Auspices of the Deputies*. Washington: Group of Ten.

Group of Thirty (G-30). 1989. *Clearance and Settlement Systems in the World's Securities Markets*. New York: Group of Thirty.

Group of Thirty (G-30), Global Derivatives Study Group. 1993. *Derivatives: Practices and Principles*. Washington: Group of Thirty.

Group of Thirty (G-30). 1994. *Derivatives: Practices and Principles: Follow-up Surveys of Industry Practice*. Washington: Group of Thirty.

Hausman, Ricardo, and Michael Gavin. 1995. "Macroeconomic Volatility in Latin America: Causes, Consequences, and Policies to Assure Stability." Unpublished. Washington: Inter-American Development Bank.

Herring, Richard, and Robert Litan. 1995. *Financial Regulation in the Global Economy*. Washington: Brookings Institution.

Hoenig, Thomas. 1996. "Rethinking Bank Regulation." *The Region* 10, no. 4 (December): 38-47 Minneapolis: Federal Reserve Bank of Minneapolis.

Honohan, Patrick. 1996. "Financial System Failures in Developing Countries: Diagnosis and Prescriptions." Unpublished. Washington: International Monetary Fund.

International Finance Corporation (IFC). 1996. *Emerging Stock Markets Factbook 1996.* Washington: International Finance Corporation.

International Monetary Fund (IMF). 1995. *International Capital Markets: Developments, Prospects, and Policy Issues.* IMF World Economic and Financial Surveys. Washington: International Monetary Fund.

International Monetary Fund (IMF). 1996a. *International Capital Markets: Developments, Prospects, and Key Policy Issues.* IMF World Economic and Financial Surveys. Washington: International Monetary Fund.

International Monetary Fund (IMF). 1996b. *World Economic Outlook.* IMF World Economic and Financial Surveys. Washington: International Monetary Fund.

International Monetary Fund (IMF). 1996c. *Standards for the Dissemination by Countries of Economic and Financial Statistics: The Special Data Dissemination Standard.* Washington: International Monetary Fund.

International Monetary Fund (IMF). 1997a. "Toward a Framework for Sound Banking" Washington: International Monetary Fund, Monetary and Exchange Affairs and Research Departments. Forthcoming.

International Monetary Fund (IMF). 1997b. *The Special Data Dissemination Standard.* http://dsbb.imf.org/overview.htm. (14 March).

Kaminsky, Graciela, and Carmen Reinhart. 1995. "The Twin Crises: The Causes of Banking and Balance of Payments Problems." Manuscript. Board of Governors of Federal Reserve System and the International Monetary Fund.

Kane, Edward. 1995. "Difficulties of Transferring Risk-Based Capital Requirements to Developing Countries." *Pacific Basin Finance Journal* 3, no. 2-3 (July): 193-216.

Kapstein, Ethan. 1991. *Supervising International Banks: Origins and Implications of the Basle Accord.* Essays in International Finance No. 185. Princeton, NJ: Princeton University, International Finance Section, Department of Economics.

Kapstein, Ethan. 1992. "Between Power and Purpose: Central Bankers and the Politics of Regulatory Convergence." *International Organization* 46, no. 1 (Winter): 265-87.

Kaufman, George. 1996a. "Lessons for Transitional and Developing Economies from US Deposit Insurance Reform." Unpublished. Chicago: Loyola University of Chicago and Federal Reserve Bank of Chicago.

Kaufman, George. 1996b. "Preventing Banking Crises in the Future: Lessons from Past Mistakes." Paper presented at the annual meeting of the Japanese Society of Monetary Economics, 25 May, Tokyo.

Kaufman, George, and Randall Kroszner. 1996. "How Should Financial Institutions and Markets Be Structured: Analysis and Options for Financial System Design." Paper presented at the IDB Conference on Safe and Sound Financial Systems: What Works for Latin America, 27-28 September, Washington.

Krivoy, Ruth. 1996. "An Agenda for Banking Crises Avoidance in Latin America." In Ricardo Hausman and Liliana Rojas-Suarez, *Banking Crises in Latin America.* Washington: Inter-American Development Bank and Johns Hopkins Press.

Lindgren, Carl-Johan, Mats Josefsson, and Jan Willem van der Vossen. 1995. "Technical Assistance in Banking Supervision in the Baltic States, Russia, and Other Countries of the Former Soviet Union." Processed. Washington: International Monetary Fund, Monetary and Exchange Affairs Department (August).

Lindgren, Carl-Johan, Gillian Garcia, and Matthew Saal. 1996. *Bank Soundness and Macroeconomic Policy.* Washington: International Monetary Fund.

Litan, Robert. 1987. *What Should Banks Do?* Washington: Brookings Institution.

Mackenzie, George, and Peter Stella. 1996. *Quasi-Fiscal Operations of Public Financial Institutions.* IMF Occasional Paper No. 142. Washington: International Monetary Fund.

Meltzer, Allan. 1995. "Sustaining Safety and Soundness: Supervision, Regulation, and Financial Reform." Unpublished. Washington: World Bank (December).

Merton, Robert. 1995. "Sources of Market Instability and Remedies." Unpublished. Cambridge, MA: Harvard University.

Mishkin, Frederick. 1994. "Preventing Financial Crisis: An International Perspective." *Manchester School of Economic and Social Studies* 62, Supplement: 1-40.

Mishkin, Frederick. 1996. "Asymmetric Information and Financial Crises: A Developing-Country Perspective." Paper presented at World Bank Annual Conference on Development Economics, 25-26 April, Washington.

Mortlock, Geof. 1996. "A New Disclosure Regime for Registered Banks." *Reserved Bank of New Zealand Bulletin* (March).

Nam, Sang Woo. 1993. "Korea's Financial Markets and Policies." Unpublished. Seoul: Korea Development Institute.

Nicholl, Peter. 1996. "Market-Based Regulation." Paper presented at the International Bank for Reconstruction and Development (IBRD) Conference on Preventing Banking Crises, April.

Padoa-Schioppa, Tommaso. 1996. "Address." Presented at the 9th International Conference of Banking Supervisors, 12-14 June, Stockholm.

Pou, Pedro. 1996. "Address." Presented at the IDB Conference on Safe and Sound Financial Systems: What Works for Latin America, 27-28 September, Washington.

Quereshi, Zia. 1996. "Globalization: New Opportunities, Tough Challenges." *Finance and Development* 33, no. 1 (January): 30-33.

Rodrik, Dani. 1995. *Why Is There Multilateral Lending?* CEPR Discussion Paper No. 1207. London: Centre for Economic Policy Research.

Rojas-Suarez, Liliana, and Steven Weisbrod. 1995. *Financial Fragility in Latin America: The 1980s and the 1990s.* IMF Occasional Paper No. 132. Washington: International Monetary Fund.

Rojas-Suarez, Liliana, and Steven Weisbrod, 1996a. "The Do's and Don'ts of Banking Crisis Management." In Ricardo Hausman and Liliana Rojas-Suarez, *Banking Crises in Latin America.* Washington: Inter-American Development Bank and Johns Hopkins Press.

Rojas-Suarez, Liliana, and Steven Weisbrod. 1996b. "Achieving Stability in Latin American Financial Markets in the Presence of Volatile Capital Flows." In Ricardo Hausman and Liliana Rojas-Suarez, *Volatile Capital Flows: Taming Their Impact on Latin America.* Washington: Inter-American Development Bank and Johns Hopkins Press.

Rojas-Suarez, Liliana, and Steven Weisbrod. 1996c. "Building Stability in Latin American Financial Markets." In Ricardo Hausman and Helmut Reisen, *Securing Stability and Growth in Latin America.* Washington: OECD Development Center and Inter-American Development Bank.

Rojas-Suarez, Liliana, and Steven Weisbrod. 1996d. "Towards an Effective Regulatory and Supervisory Framework in Latin America." Paper presented at the IDB Conference on Safe and Sound Financial Systems: What Works for Latin America, 27-28 September, Washington.

Seidman, William. 1996. "Lessons Learned, Challenges Ahead." Paper presented at the Nikkin 7th Special Seminar on International Finance, 18 September, Tokyo.

Sheng, Andrew. 1996. *Bank Restructuring: Lessons from the 1980s.* Washington: World Bank.

Summers, Lawrence. 1996. "Strengthening Emerging Market Financial Systems: An Agenda for Action." *Treasury News* of the US Department of the Treasury (27 September).

Sundararajan, Vasudevan, and Tomas Balino. 1991. *Banking Crises: Cases and Issues.* Washington: International Monetary Fund.

US Office of the Comptroller of the Currency. *Quarterly Journal.* Washington: GPO.

White, Lawrence. 1996. "Competition versus Harmonization: An Overview of International Regulation of Financial Services." In Claude Barfield, *International Financial Markets: Harmonization versus Competition*. Washington: American Enterprise Institute.

White, William. 1996. *International Agreements in the Area of Banking and Finance: Accomplishments and Outstanding Issues*. BIS Working Paper No. 38. Basle: Bank for International Settlements.

Williamson, John. 1995. *What Role for Currency Boards?* POLICY ANALYSES IN INTERNATIONAL ECONOMICS 40. Washington: Institute for International Economics.

World Bank. 1997. *The Road to Financial Integration: Private Capital Flows to Developing Countries*. Washington: World Bank. Forthcoming.

Other Publications from the Institute for International Economics

Reforming World Agricultural Trade
Twenty-nine Professionals from Seventeen Countries/1988
ISBN paper 0-88132-088-9   42 pp.

8 Economic Relations Between the United States and Korea:
   Conflict or Cooperation?
   Thomas O. Bayard and Soo-Gil Young, editors/January 1989
ISBN paper 0-88132-068-4   192 pp.

WORKS IN PROGRESS

Liberalizing Financial Services
Michael Aho and Pierre Jacquet

Trade, Jobs, and Income Distribution
William R. Cline

China's Entry to the World Economy
Richard N. Cooper

Corruption and the Global Economy
Kimberly Ann Elliott

Economic Sanctions After the Cold War
Kimberly Ann Elliott, Gary C. Hufbauer and Jeffrey J. Schott

Trade and Labor Standards
Kimberly Ann Elliott and Richard Freeman

Regional Trading Blocs in the World Economic System
Jeffrey A. Frankel

Transatlantic Economic Cooperation: A Strategic Agenda
Ellen Frost

Forecasting Financial Crises: Early Warning Signs for Emerging Markets
Morris Goldstein and Carmen Reinhart

Overseeing Global Capital Markets
Morris Goldstein and Peter Garber

Global Competition Policy
Edward M. Graham and J. David Richardson

The Global Impact of Economic and Monetary Union
C. Randall Henning

Prospects for Western Hemisphere Free Trade
Gary Clyde Hufbauer and Jeffrey J. Schott

The Future of U.S. Foreign Aid
Carol Lancaster

The Economics of Korean Unification
Marcus Noland

The Case for Trade: A Modern Reconsideration
J. David Richardson

Measuring the Cost of Protection in China
Zhang Shuguang, Zhang Yansheng, and Wan Zhongxin

Who's Bashing Whom? Trade Conflict in High-Technology Industries, Second Edition
Laura D'Andrea Tyson

Canadian customers can order from the Institute or from either:

RENOUF BOOKSTORE
1294 Algoma Road
Ottawa, Ontario K1B 3W8
Telephone: 613 741-4333
Fax: 613 741-5439

LA LIBERTÉ
3020 chemin Sainte-Foy
Quebec G1X 3V6
Telephone: 418 658-3763
Fax: 800 567-5449

Visit our website at: http:/ / www.iie.com
E-mail address: orders@iie.com